Python Programming for School Students

Suitable for class X to XII students

Mahendra Verma
IIT Kanpur

First paperback edition September 2021

ISBN: 978-93-91374-63-1 (paperback)

To

My dear sister Kesari Verma

CONTENTS

Preface

Who is this book meant for?

Even though Python programming is easy, it does require certain preparation in mathematics and logic. Therefore, I believe that students of classes X to XII will enjoy this book. However, younger students too could attempt to study parts of the book.

Some topics of the book are somewhat difficult. Still, I recommend that the students should learn them by spending more time. If you find some chapters or sections (e.g., prime numbers) to be too difficult, you could skip them and move on. Part-II of the book deals with Algebra, geometry, and a bit of statistics. This optional part may interest mathematics students of class XI and XII.

How to use this book?

Programming is like painting or swimming. We learn these skills by practice. Hence, I strongly urge the students to practice coding, rather than simply reading the book. Open your computer and type the statements of the book and run the codes. Do as many exercises as possible! For your convenience, the codes of the book, as well as video lectures and PPTs, will be made available on the website https://sites.google.com/view/py-school.

Acknowledgements

This book is a simpler version of my Computational Physics course at IIT Kanpur. I am grateful to the course TAs (teaching assistants), especially Soumyadeep Chatterjee, Abhishek Kumar, Manohar Sharma, and the class students for suggestions and comments.

Next, thanks to Python developers for creating wonderful

programming environment, that too for free! I am grateful to *Anancoda* for the free Python distribution. This book was created effortlessly using *Scrivener*.

I am also thankful to my sister Late Kesari Verma, Rahul Garg, Prachi Garg, Shalini Tiwari, Richa Khestrapal, and my family members for the encouragement to complete this project; and to Ishika Sinha, Vikas Gupta, and Dhruv Garg for a careful proofread of the book. The cover page was designed by Adhyyan Books.

I gratefully acknowledge Wikipedia and Wikieducator for Figures 2, 4, 5, 35, and 55 of the book.

Feedback request

I request the readers to send their comments and feedback to me at mkv@iitk.ac.in. Even though I have tried hard to make the book error free, I am sure some bugs still remain. I will be grateful if the errors are brought to my attention.

Mahendra Verma

Part One

General Introduction to Computers

"The digital revolution is far more significant than the invention of writing or even of printing."
— *Douglas Engelbart*

CHAPTER ONE

INTRODUCTION TO COMPUTERS

Synopsis

"I do not fear computers. I fear lack of them."
— Isaac Asimov

Computers are everywhere and they impact all walks of lives. This chapter gives a brief introduction to computer hardware and software.

1.1 Computer Hardware

A computer is a digital device that stores and processes data, typically digital data. In addition, a computer can be programmed to perform different tasks—web browsing, email, running programs, playing music and movies, controlling a car, etc.

Let us illustrate the functioning of a computer using an example. We want to build a pizza cutter that cuts a pizza into required number of pieces. This machine has several important features:

1. Input: Full-size pizza and the number of required pieces.
2. Storage: Here we place a full-size pizza that is to be cut into smaller pieces.
3. Output: Dispenser for the pizza pieces.
4. Processor: This unit cuts the pizza to smaller pieces.

A schematic diagram of the machine is illustrated in Figure 1.

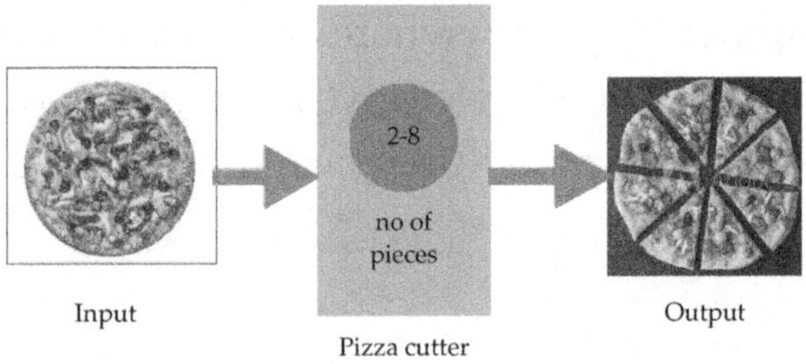

Figure 1: A pizza cutter takes a full-size pizza, cuts it into the required number of pieces, and delivers them.

The working of the above machine is as follows:

1. Insert the pizza, and input the number of required pieces.
2. Cut the full pizza into the required number of pieces.
3. Dispense the cut pieces.

We could iterate this process to cut more pizzas. The above pizza cutter is programmable because we can change the required number of pieces. Vending machine too is a programmable device. However, a hammer or a knife is not a programmable device; these machines can do only one thing.

After this simple example, we briefly describe a computer. At present, most people use laptops, hence we will detail this device. You have seen a desktop computer or a laptop. Other kinds of computers will be mentioned at the end of the section. In the following discussion, we will describe a laptop in some detail.

Exterior of a laptop

The exterior of a laptop has a screen, a keyboard, a trackpad, a camera, and several ports. The ports are typically on the sides of the laptop. See Figure 2 for an illustration. Let us describe the above parts briefly:

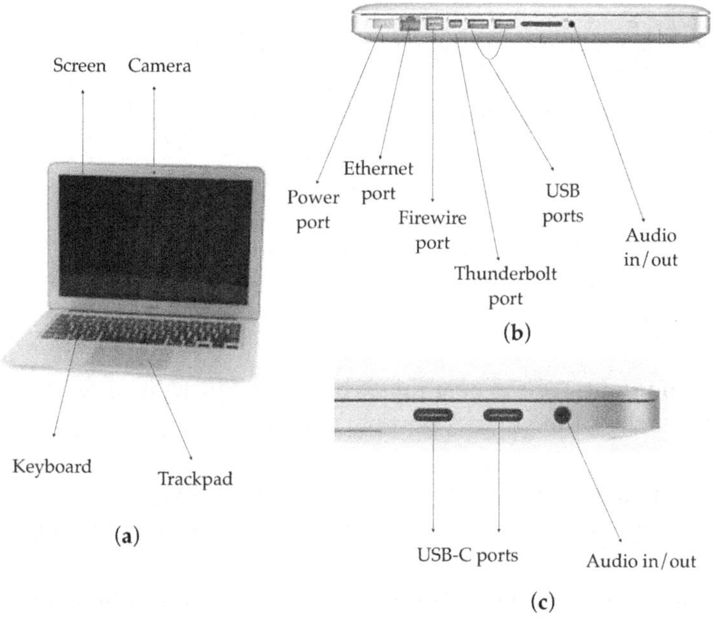

Figure 2: (a) Laptop; (b,c) Ports of a laptop. Adapted from figures of wikipedia.org. Source: Wikipedia.

Keyboard: A computer takes inputs or commands from a user via a keyboard. A computer program is also entered in the laptop using the keyboard.

Screen: The computer displays its output on the screen, which is also called a *display monitor*. The output could be text, images, or videos coming from a computer program, an internet, or a keyboard. A screen could exhibit multiple outputs on different windows. For example, your could read your email, browse the internet, and watch a movie in three different windows on the monitor.

Trackpad: Trackpad is an input device of a laptop. We can reach various parts of a screen using a trackpad.

Camera: We can either take a picture or record a video using the laptop's camera. Note that the image or video of the camera could be an input to a program, e.g., Whatsapp or a video-editing program.

Now, a brief on the laptop ports shown in Figure 2(b).

Power port: The port is for charging the battery located inside the laptop.

USB port: Using a *universal serial bus* (*USB*) port, we can either copy data from a pendrive to a laptop or transfer data from a laptop to a pendrive. In addition, cameras, scanners, and printers can be connected to the laptop using a USB port.

Audio in/out: We can hear music or record music by inserting an audio cable to the Audio in/out port of the laptop.

Firewire and Thunderbolt ports: These ports are useful for connecting the laptop to external display devices, such as a TV or a projector.

Ethernet port: A laptop can receive/send data from/to an internet via an ethernet cable attached to an ethernet port. However, most modern laptops do not have ethernet port and they use only a wireless connection for internet data transmission. The wireless device resides inside a laptop.

Some of the recent laptops avoid multiple ports mentioned above. Instead, they have several USB-C ports (see Figure 2(c)) that is used for charging the laptop, as well as for connecting to a USC-C hub. The USB-C hub has many ports for connecting to pendrive, external monitors, TV, projector, ethernet, etc.

The laptop connects to the outside world using these input/output components (keyboard, monitor, touchpad, cameras) and ports. This is similar to how an animal interacts with the outside world using eyes, ears, mouth, nose, etc. Clearly, the input data goes inside the laptop. What does a laptop do with this data? To answer this question, we need to get inside the laptop.

The world inside a laptop

Inside a laptop, data is processed in a *processor* (also called *central processing unit* or CPU). For example, numbers are multiplied inside the processor. In addition, the numbers are stored temporarily in the *memory*. Also, the input/output devices talk to the processor and memory via *I/O controller*. The above units—the processor, memory, and I/O controller—are placed on a printed circuit board (PCB) called *Motherboard* or *logicboard*, which is illustrated in Figure 3. The motherboard resides inside a laptop.

In addition to the above, a laptop also contains a hard disk, a battery, a wireless device, and a camera. The inputs to the laptop arrive at the processor, who operates on these inputs and sends appropriate outputs (for example, message to the screen). When we run a program, the data and programs are stored inside the memory from where they flow to the processor. The processor runs the programs and sends the results to the memory. Note that the data in the memory is temporary; it will disappear when the laptop is shutdown. Therefore, we need to save important data from the memory to the hard disk.

Let us get a deeper perspective on various units.

Processor: A processor performs logical and arithmetic operations on the data. For example, the processor can add two numbers A and B. The processor, also called *central processing unit* (CPU), is the most complex and critical component of a computer, and it can perform billions of arithmetic operations per second. It is like the brain of a human being. An important thing to note is that during the addition *A+B*, the numbers *A*, *B*, and *A+B* are stored in a small memory, called *registers*, of the CPU.

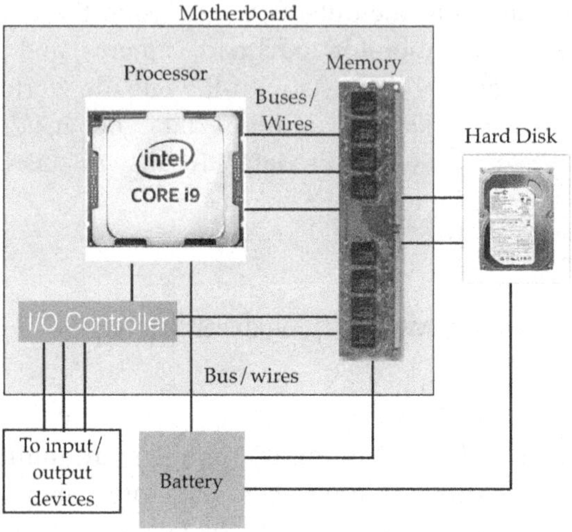

Figure 3: A schematic diagram exhibiting internals of a laptop: Processor, Memory, Hard Disk, Battery. Some components of the figure are taken from wikipedia.org.

Memory: The data and programs reside in *memory* (vertical strip inside the motherboard of Figure 3), also called *random access memory* (RAM). This memory is temporary because it is active only when the laptop is powered on.

Hard disk: This is a permanent storage. The program and data remain in the hard disk even when the laptop is turned off. When we turn on the laptop, the programs and data are transferred from the hard disk to the RAM. The processor operates on these data using various programs. Hence, the processor, RAM, and hard disk continuously interact with each other.

Buses: The above devices are connected via thin wires called *buses*.

Battery: The laptop battery powers all the units.

Wireless device, camera, trackpad hardware, microphone too reside inside the laptop. Also note that printers, scanners, external cameras, and microphones, are typically connected to a laptop via USB ports.

The intricate parts discussed above indicate that a laptop is a complex entity, which is realised as a result of around one hundred years of research and development. Also note the clear segregation of CPU and memory in the computer. Contrast this segregation in a computer with the human brain where data processing and storage often occur in the same region. Some modern computers mimic the above aspect of a human brain.

Different types of computers

Computers come in different variants, but their basic design remains the same. We list various computer systems below.

Desktop: Desktops are used in offices and homes as immobile computers. Compared to laptops, these machines have more powerful and power consuming components. Desktops often use a mouse in place of a trackpad. See Figure 4 for an illustration.

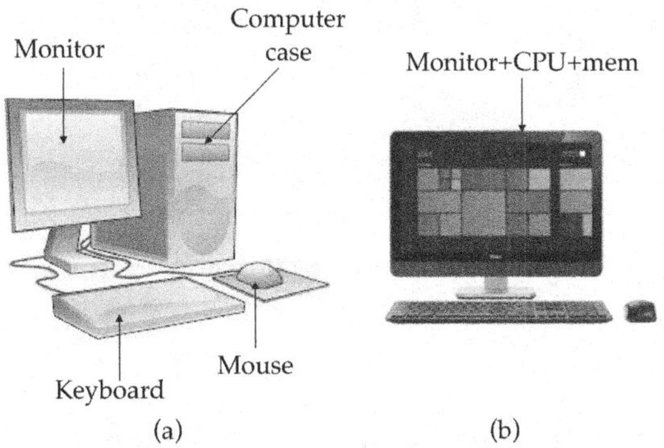

Figure 4: Desktop computers. In (b), CPU, memory, hard disk reside behind the monitor screen. Source wikipedia.org.

In Figure 4(a), the CPU, memory, and hard disk reside in the computer case, which is also called *tower* or *computer chassis*. Monitor, keyboard, and mouse are connected to the tower. However, many new desktops combine the monitor and internal hardware, such as CPU, memory, and hard disk (see Figure 4(b)).

Computer workstations: Workstations have stronger processors and larger memory than desktops. Hence, they are more powerful than desktops. These machines have much larger display monitors for data visualisation.

Supercomputers: Complex tasks, such as banking, weather predictions, traffic management, etc. cannot be performed on a laptop or a desktop. For the above operations, we employ supercomputers, which are collections of many powerful processors with huge memory. Fugaku, the fastest supercomputer as on November 2020, contains 7 million processors, and it can perform 442×10^{15} arithmetic operations per second (see Figure 5). We skip discussion on supercomputers because they are too complex to be covered here.

Figure 5: Fugaku, the fastest supercomputer of 2020. Source: wikipedia.org. Work of Hiroko Hama; reprinted under the agreement of CC BY-SA 4.0 license.

Mobiles and tablets: Mobiles and tablets too are computers because they have processors and memory, and they perform similar operations as a laptop. However, the components of a mobile or a tablet are much less powerful than those of a laptop. Also, these devices consume much less power. A mobile cannot perform complex and long computations, but a laptop can.

Gaming devices: Gaming devices are computers as well. They contain fast processors and powerful graphic cards for rendering high-resolution animations and videos.

Embedded computers: Small computers are embedded in many home devices and automobiles. For example, the health of the engine and brakes of a car are monitored by an embedded computer in the car. Rasberry Pi (https://www.raspberrypi.org) is a popular general-purpose cheap computer. Self-driving cars have more powerful computers inside.

Once a computer has been assembled, its parts mentioned above are unchangeable. That is, the CPU and display remain as they are (unless they are replaced). Due to these reasons, these parts are called *hardware* of a computer. On the contrary, the programs and data of the laptop change all the time, hence they are called *software*. In the next section, we discuss software of a computer.

****

Conceptual questions

1. Why do we have two different types of memory devices inside the laptop: RAM and hard disk? What are the differences in their functioning?
2. Identify programmable devices around you.

Exercises

1. Take a picture of a flower and store it your laptop.
2. Record a song on your laptop.
3. Read how computers have evolved over time.
4. What are the differences between a desktop and a laptop, and those between a mobile and laptop?

5. Compare the power requirements of a generic laptop, a generic desktop, and a mobile phone.

1.2 Computer Software and Python

A powered-up laptop is alive, that is, it is aware of its CPU, memory, and input/output units—the screen, keyboard, trackpad, etc. For example, a laptop responds to the inputs from the keyboard; it print a document on the printer; it executes user programs; etc. The program that keeps the computer alive is called *Operating System* or *OS*.

When a computer is in a power-off state, the OS resides in the hard disk. As soon as a computer is turned on, the computer is partially awake. For a complete functionality of the computer, the OS is loaded into the RAM with the help of the processor. After this, the computer is fully awake, and it is ready to take orders and run other programs, such as Word processor, Web browser, Mail, etc.

Computer softwares are many. They range from small ones to very large and complex ones. We do not describe them here, except that we list some softwares that you would have used.

Most of you would have used internet browsers—Firefox mozilla, Safari, Microsoft Edge, etc. An internet browser is an example of a software. Note that *browsing* technically means reading and scanning through data. Other prominent softwares are email readers and Microsoft Word that helps us write documents. Image-processing softwares capture images and enhance their quality by tweaks. In addition, there are softwares for video editing. All the *apps* (short form for *application*) of your mobile are softwares.

Python, which is the topic of this book, is also a software. Using this software, we can perform the following set of applications:

1. Numerical and scientific computing; Data analysis
2. Working with big data; Machine learning
3. Image processing; Run audio and video applications
4. Interface to experimental devices and control (e.g., temperature measurement)
5. Internet programming

Python is one of the most popular languages at present. In this book we will show how to write programs using Python.

Python in comparison to other programming languages

A *computer program* (or *computer code*) is a list of instructions written in a structured manner. It has some resemblance with human language (typically English). A C program to print "Hello World!" is given below. Here, the function *printf* prints whatever appears inside the parenthesis ().

```
#include <stdio.h>
int main() {
   printf("Hello, World!");
}
```

A C compiler converts the above program to a *binary code*, which is a set of instructions written in 0's and 1's. The binary code is executed by the CPU.

There are many programming languages, such as C, C++, Java, Fortran, Python, etc. Python is the simplest programming language among all of them. This is why it is recommended as the first computer language to learn. Many school children are learning this programming language at an early age.

In spite of its simplicity, Python is a very powerful language. In fact, Python's simplicity is its virtue; many complex codes have been built over its simple constructs. Python is used heavily for scientific programming, data analysis, machine learning, internet programming, instrumentation, etc. We will illustrate some of these ideas later in this book.

However, Python programs have certain deficiencies. A Python program is typically slower than its C or C++ counterparts. But, A Python code is much shorter and easier to develop than its C/C++ equivalent.

There is another important distinction between Python and C/C++. Python is an interpreter language. That is, Python (to be precise, Python interpreter) talks to us interactively. A typical Python interaction is as follows:

```
In [1]: 2+3
Out[1]: 5
```

```
In [2]: x=10

In [3]: print(x**2)
100
```

We write 2+3 in the input line, to which, Python produces 5 as output (see *Out* [1]). We declare x as a variable with a value of 10 (*In* [2]) and ask Python to print(x**2). Python immediately prints 100. This continuous interaction with the computer is very beneficial while learning how to program. You can test your idea or code segment right away! Due to such an interactive feature, Python is called an *interpreter language*.

In C and C++, we have to write the complete computer program and then submit it to the computer. The program is converted to a binary code by the *compiler*. After this, the computer executes the binary code and gives an output. Due to this stage-wise process (program writing → compilation → program execution), such languages are called *compiler languages*.

Note that a Python program also converts a Python code to a binary code, but it is done after each step (e.g., after *In* [1], *In* [2]). Clearly, finding an error in a large C code is much more cumbersome than that in a Python code, which can be developed piece by piece. This is another advantage of Python, especially when learning how to code for the first time.

Python modules

A major positive aspect of Python is its vast libraries that includes *Numpy, Matplotlib, Scipy, Math, Pandas, Sympy,* etc. There are specialised Python libraries for chemistry, astronomy, machine learning, etc. Technically, Python libraries are called *modules*. A brief description of some of the important modules are given below.

- *Numpy*: *Numpy* is a short form for *Numerical Python*. This module contains mathematical functions, such as *sin, cos, log, sqrt*, etc. Also, *numpy* contains functions for array operations.

- *Math*: This module contains various mathematical functions.

Some math functions, e.g., trigonometric and logarithm functions, are common between *math* and *numpy* modules. However, some other functions, e.g., *factorial,* exist only in the *Math* library (not in *Numpy*).

- *Matplotlib*: This Python module helps create beautiful plots.

- *Pandas*: This module is useful for data analysis, plotting, etc.

- *Turtle*: Using *Turtle* module, we can create geometrical objects.

In this introductory book we will deal with *Numpy, Math, Matplotlib,* and *Turtle* libraries only.

The best way to learn programming is to actually program. It is like swimming, which can be learnt only by jumping into a pool. No amount of theorising will help you learn coding. We strongly urge you to shed fear and laziness, and start programming.

Fortunately, many excellent Python interpreters are available for free. You can install them on your laptop or desktop and learn Python. You can also write Python programs on the web-based apps, such as *Collab* and *Jupyter Notebooks*. We will list four Python platforms in the next sections. You can choose any one of them. However, I recommend installing *Anaconda Python* on your laptop or desktop.

****

Conceptual questions

1. What is the difference between computer hardware and software? Illustrate your answer using examples.
2. Python is a preferred language for first timers. Why?

1.3 Python in Your Machine

Basic Python or Core Python comes preinstalled in Macintosh and Linux distributions. However, you need to install it in Windows system. Python installation is very easy. You can download it from https://www.python.org/downloads/ and install it locally on your laptop/desktop/workstation. We recommend installation of Python 3.

We start the Python interpreter on a Linux or Windows terminal using *python* command at the prompt. We can execute Python statements, e.g., 2+3/4, after that. A typical output appears as follows:

```
(base) ~/python
Python 3.7.4 (default, Aug 13 2019, 15:17:50)
[Clang 4.0.1 (tags/RELEASE_401/final)] :: Anaconda, Inc.
on darwin
Type "help", "copyright", "credits" or "license" for more
information.
>>> 2+3/4
2.75
>>>
```

However, the plain Python interpreter can execute *only* core Python statements including basic data structures like *list*. But, more complex structures such as *numpy arrays* are not included in core Python. Also, the core Python does not contain many scientific libraries, such as trigonometric functions, matrix solvers, etc. For the same, you will need to separately download *Numpy, Scipy, Matplotlib, Math, Pandas,* and other Python modules and install them separately.

An attractive alternative is to install a large package that contains basic Python and all the modules. One such package is *Anaconda Python*. As the name suggests, Anaconda Python (a giant serpent, surpassing Python) contains almost everything of Python. In this section, we describe the installation and some features of Anaconda Python.

Installation of Anaconda Python

Anaconda Python (version 3.8) is available for free download (for individuals) from Anaconda's website (https://www.anaconda.com). The file is around ½ gigabytes, so it may take a while for downloading (depending on your internet speed).

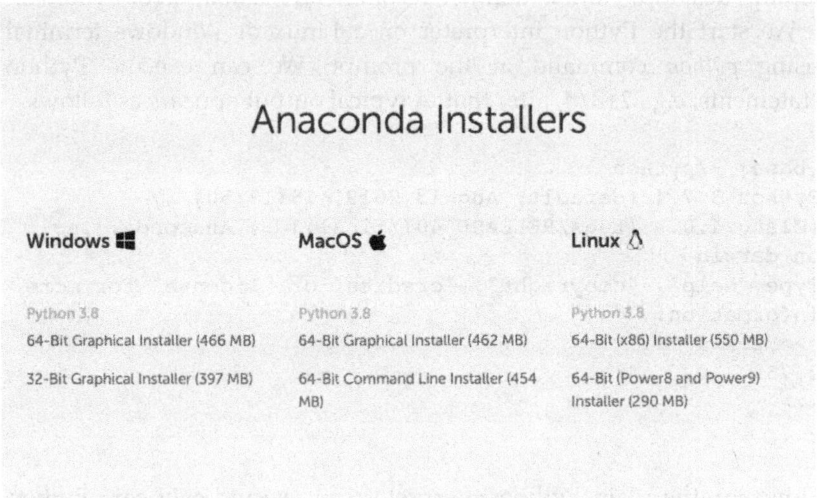

Figure 6: A screenshot for Ananconda installers. From https://www.anaconda.com.

The steps for Python installation are as follows. You could also refer to the video tutorial (https://www.youtube.com/watch?v=5mDYijMfSzs). Here we list the steps for installation on a windows laptop/PC.

1. Visit https://www.anaconda.com/products/individual. It leads to the screen shown in Figure 6.
2. Click the link on *64-Bit Graphical Installer*. In Windows system, this will download the .exe installer.
3. Open and run the .exe installer.
4. It installs the packages. In Windows, the default directory is C:\ProgramData\Python3.
5. This process puts many packages including GUI called *spyder* in the above directory.

On a Mac or Linux computer/laptop, use the corresponding 64-Bit Graphical Installers. On a Mac, double click on the downloaded *dmg* file and follow the instructions. Anaconda3 is installed in $home/opt/anaconda3 directory. If the *path* has been set properly, Python is ready for execution on a *terminal*. You can open a terminal by clicking *Terminal* that resides inside the Applications/Utilities folder in Mac.

On the terminal, at the command prompt ($ sign below; note that the command prompt may be different on your computer), type:

$ipython --pylab

You will see the following output:

```
Python 3.7.4 (default, Aug 13 2019, 15:17:50)
Type 'copyright', 'credits' or 'license' for more information
IPython 7.8.0 -- An enhanced Interactive Python. Type '?' for help.
Using matplotlib backend: MacOSX

In [1]: █
```

Now you can start typing Python statements. A sample is here:

```
In [1]: 2+3
Out[1]: 5
```

Here, *In* [1] contains an input to the Python interpreter, while *Out* [1] contains the output by the interpreter. Thus, *ipython* provides an interactive environment. Using *pylab,* we can compute mathematical functions, such as $sin(x)$, $log(x)$, as well as plot the data.

Python modules are quite complex for a beginner. That is why we recommend *ipython* with *pylab* option. When we type *ipython --pylab* on a command window, Python automatically imports *numpy* and *matplotlib*. After this, we can easily use all the mathematical and plotting functions without worrying about which library they belong to. For example, at the prompt we can type $sqrt(4)$ that returns 2. We can manage like this till Chapter Seven. In Chapter Eight we show how to use modules in your programs.

You could also run Anaconda Python using a GUI (graphical user interface) called *Spyder*. To start *Spyder,* first launch *Anaconda-Navigator,* after which click the *spyder* package. You could also start *Spyder* from the terminal by typing *spyder*. As a result, a GUI with three windows—*Editor, Help,* and *Ipython* consoles—is launched. These windows appear in the left, upper right, and lower right of the GUI (see Figure 7). We can type the Python statements in the Ipython console (lower right).

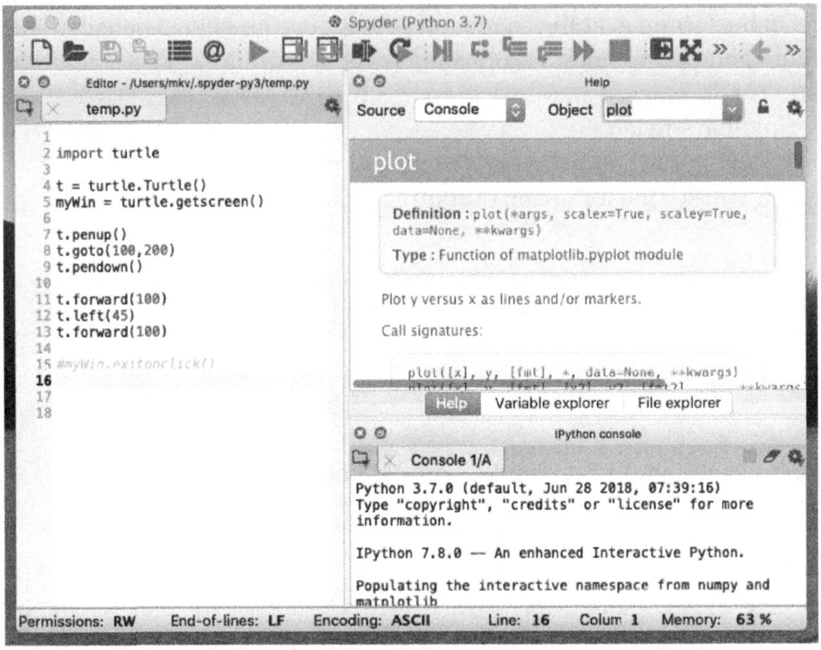

Figure 7: Spyder GUI with *Editor, Help,* and *Ipython* consoles.

To import mathematical and plotting functions in *Spyder,* type the following lines in the beginning itself.

```
from numpy import *
from matplotlib.pyplot import *
from math import *
```

After this, you can use all the mathematical and plotting functions.

Creating a Python file using an editor

We can write small Python program in *ipython* window itself.

However, it is cumbersome to type codes with 10 or more lines on a terminal. We employ text editors—*Gedit, Vi, Vim, IDLE, Atom, Sublime, Xcode,* etc.—in such a scenario. We recommend *Sublime Text* (https://www.sublimetext.com), which is available for Windows, Mac, and Linux.

Typing in *Sublime* is very easy. A screenshot of a Python code typed in Sublime is shown below (Figure 8):

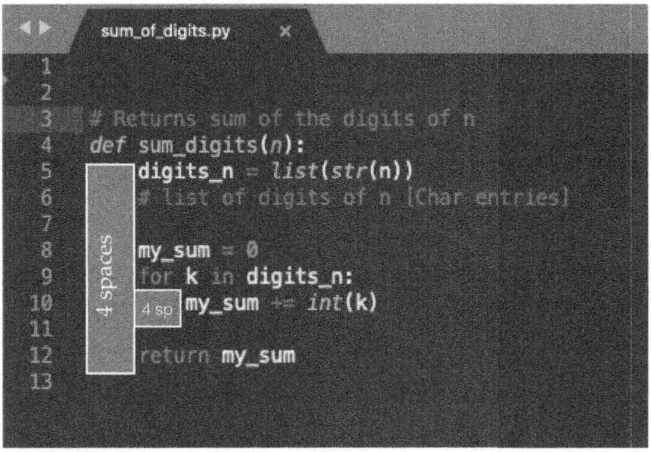

Figure 8: A snapshot of a Python file *sum_of_digits.py* created using the Sublime editor.

Note that a Python program needs to be properly *indented*. Indentation is a must for Python codes! That is, we need to place an appropriate number of spaces in each line. Lines 5, 6, 8, 9, and 12 contain 4 spaces, while line 10 has 8 spaces. The code will not run if these spaces are not provided. Note that we can use any number of spaces (rather than 4), but the number of spaces must be the same for all the statements of a code block.

This file needs to be saved using a file name. By default, a file is saved in the same folder in which *Ipython* is running. Also, Python files have *.py* extension. We execute the statements of this file using a command, *run filename*. In the following example, we execute the file *sum_of_digits.py*. Note that the function *sum_digits(n)* is defined in the file, hence it can be used after the execution of the file.

```
In [115]: run sum_of_digits.py
```

```
In [116]: sum_digits(128)
  Out[116]: 11
```

With this we end our discussion on Anaconda Python.

1.4 Python Notebooks

You can run Python on online platforms called *Python Notebooks*. This way, you can avoid the trouble of installing Python on your computer. In this section we will describe two python notebooks—*Colab* and *Jupyter*.

Working with Colab

Type https://colab.research.google.com/notebooks/ on your browser. The browser pops up the following window (see Figure 9).

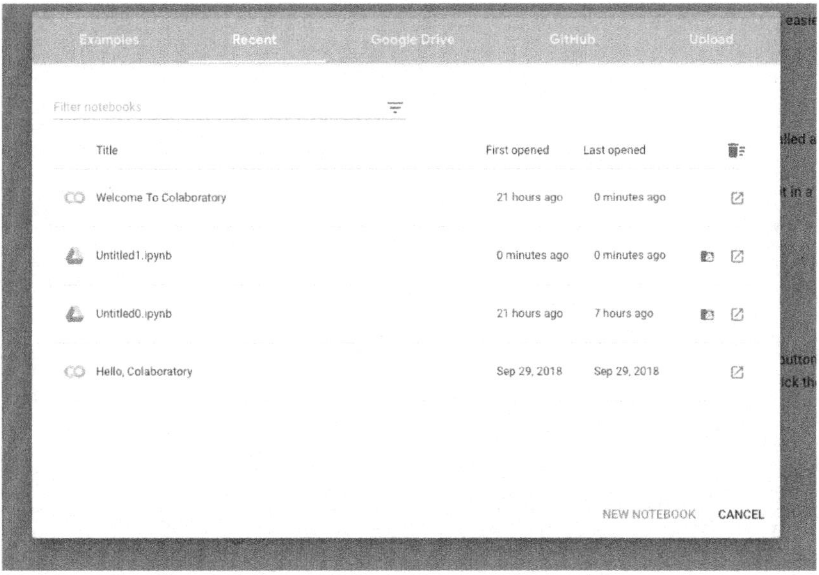

Figure 9: Starting *collab notebook.* A clip from https://colab.research.google.com/.

Click on *Welcome to Collaboratory* after which another page opens where we click on the *New Notebook* under the *File* menu. Save that as *my first python.ipynb*. Here, we can write Python codes. See Figure 10 for an illustration.

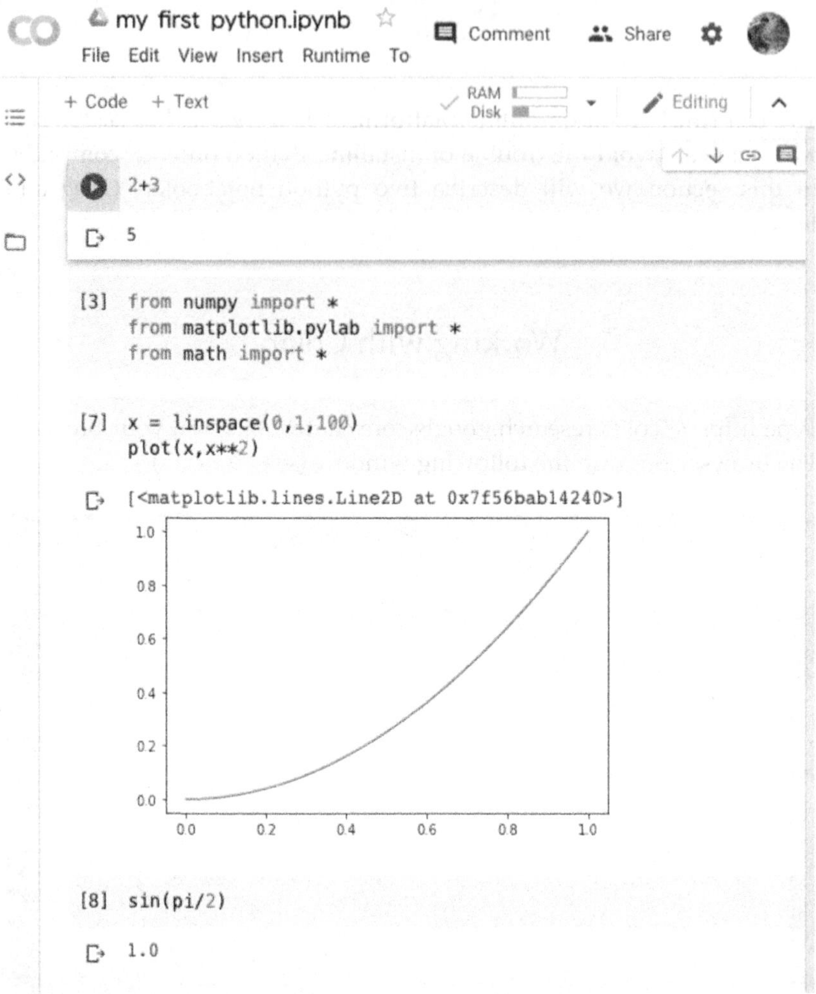

Figure 10: Working with *collab notebook.* A clip from https://colab.research.google.com/.

One can easily navigate in a Python Notebook. For example, + *code* button is used for creating new lines of Python codes. The ▶ (play) button to the left of the code is used to run the code. We can save the notebook using the *save* option in the *File* dropdown.

As discussed in the previous sections, we import mathematical and plotting functions by typing the following statements at the top of the notebook.

```
from numpy import *
from matplotlib.pyplot import *
from math import *
```

The codes discussed in this book could be run on *collab* notebooks. Refer to Collab's documentation and video tutorials for more information.

Jupyter too offers a Python notebook platform, which is briefed below.

Working with Jupyter notebook

Visit https://jupyter.org/try and click on Try Classic Notebook. After that, we click *Notebook Basics* that pops up an ipython window in which we can type Python commands. A screenshot of the window is shown below (see Figure 11).

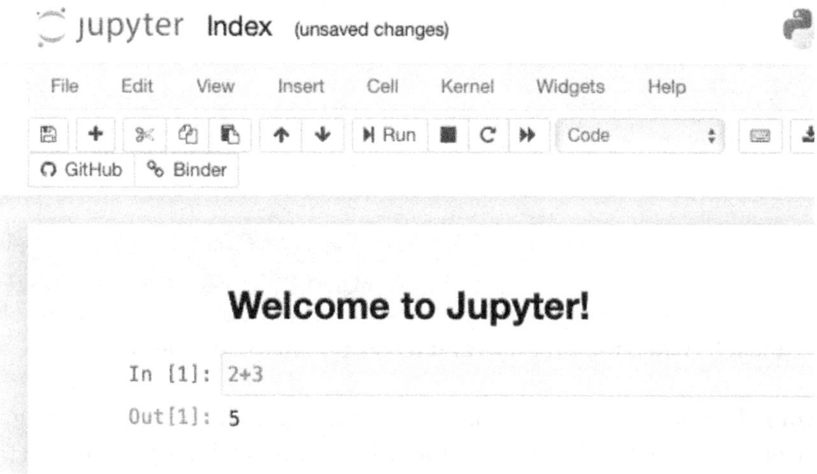

Figure 11: Working with *Jupyter notebook*. A clip from https://jupyter.org.

The functions of collab and Jupyter platforms are very similar, hence we do not detail them here.

Working with Prutor

An interesting Python tutor named *Prutor* has been developed in IIT Kanpur by Prof. Amey Karkare and his team. *Prutor,* a short form for *Program Tutor,* is an intelligent tutoring system for programming. *Prutor,* which is installed on a server, hosts many programming exercises. A student can login to the server via a web browser and solve the problems on the Prutor platform itself. On submission, Prutor evaluates the solution of a problem against given test cases and provides the student an immediate feedback on the program's correctness (whether the program's output matches with the expected answer). In case of error, you need to revise your solution. A screenshot of a programming session on Prutor is shown in Figure 12.

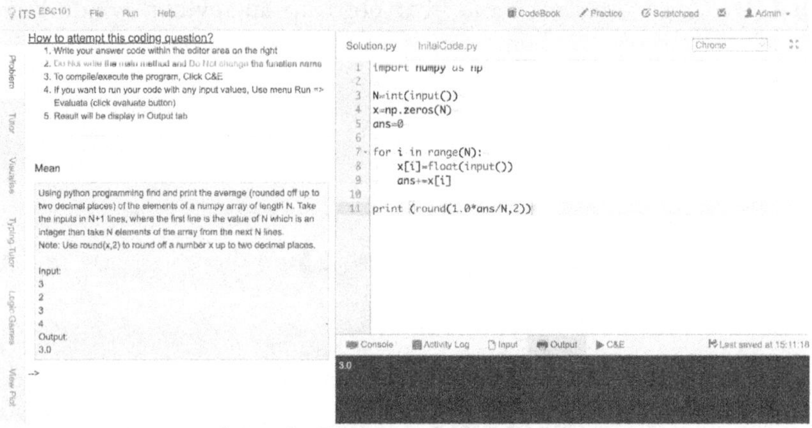

Figure 12: A screenshot of a *Prutor* session. The problem statement is on the left, while the program and its output are on the right.

Thus, Prutor provides automated tutoring for Python programming. Prutor is hosted at https://prutor.ai by Prutor Online Academy, IIT Kanpur. Prutor is also available for C programming language. A Prutor course is being designed based on this book (https://prutor.ai/mkvatiitkanpur/#)

1.5 Applications of Computers

We end this chapter with an overview of various applications of computers in our society.

- **At Home**: At present, almost everyone uses a mobile, which is a mini computer. We go to the internet for information; use email and social media applications—Facebook and Twitter; and play computer games. At homes, most appliances—TV, refrigerator, ACs—are controlled by embedded processors inside them.

- **Entertainment**: Movies, music, and photography have gone digital at present. They are stored in digital form in a computer, as well as processed digitally using a computer. Computers play critical role in social media (e.g., Twitter and Facebook).

- **Education**: Books and education contents (including this book) are generated using computers. Internet has a wealth of information that are useful in education. Online or virtual lectures have became possible due to computers and internet.

- **Business**: Banking sectors employ computers in a big way. ATMs are computers that vend money. Electronic transactions are made possible by computers. Other daily business applications involving computers are e-ticketing, e-shopping, etc. Also, stock markets employ many computers for various operations.

- **Automobiles**: Many operations inside car, trains, aeroplanes are performed by computers. For example, heat sensors and processors warn a driver if the engine is too hot. Global Positioning System (GPS) helps us navigate on the roads.

- **Industry**: Most industrial operations are automated now. For example, in the steel industry, the injection, melting, and mixing of ores are controlled by computers. Many dangerous tasks, e.g., cleaning a nuclear furnace, are performed by robots.

- **Science and Technology**: We rely on computers for many critical applications. For example, weather forecasting is performed by supercomputers. We employ computers for designing new drugs, efficient automobiles and aeroplanes, construction of large structures, etc. Spacecrafts and satellites rely heavily on computers.

The above examples are only a fraction of computer applications.

****

Exercises

1. List all computer applications used in your school.
2. Identify home appliances at your house that rely on computers.
3. List the mobile apps that you use.

CHAPTER TWO
PROBLEM SOLVING USING COMPUTERS

Synopsis

"A computer once beat me at chess, but it was no match for me at kickboxing." — Emo Philips

"The good news about computers is that they do what you tell them to do. The bad news is that they do what you tell them to do." — Ted Nelson

In this chapter we describe some important and simple programming algorithms.

2.1 Examples of Computational Problems

Problem solving using computers requires very different skills compared to those involved in science, mathematics, or history. This is because computers can perform only clearly-stated logical steps. In contrast, as a human being, we can answer a physics question using rational arguments and existing theories. For example, in physics, we can explain why things fall under gravity, but present computers cannot answer such question or create physical arguments. Similarly, a human teacher can correct subjective questions (like, why things fall under gravity?), but such a task is not yet possible by a computer. It is claimed that *Artificial Intelligence* (*AI*) can help bridge this gap, but we are still far from designing a computer (hardware and software) that can match human intelligence.

At present, to solve a particular problem on a computer, we have to provide it with all the logical steps. A step-by-step process to solve a problem is called an *algorithm*. In the following, we list several simple algorithms.

Example 1: Find the tallest student in a class.

Solution: A logical procedure to solve this problem is as follows. We start with the first student and compare her with the second one. We pick taller among the two. After this, we compare this student with the third student and pick taller among the two. Continue this process till the end. The final comparison will give us the tallest student in the class. See Figure 13 for an illustration where we compare four students, whose names are A, B, C, and D.

A computer can perform the above task quite easily. It can compare heights (compare two numbers) and go from one student to the next. In Section 9.2, we will write a Python program for the same.

We may believe that some people can solve this problem using a quick glance at all the students. However, the present understanding of science is that our brains too performs similar comparisons as above. But, a human brain may not perform this task sequentially, that is, one after the other; it may divide the students into clusters (e.g., rows), and then compare the heights of the student in clusters simultaneously. After that the brain may compare the tallest students of each cluster and figure out the tallest student in the class. Such operations are called *parallel processing*. Also, note that a human being may make a mistake in his/her identification if several students have similar heights. A computer will never make such mistakes.

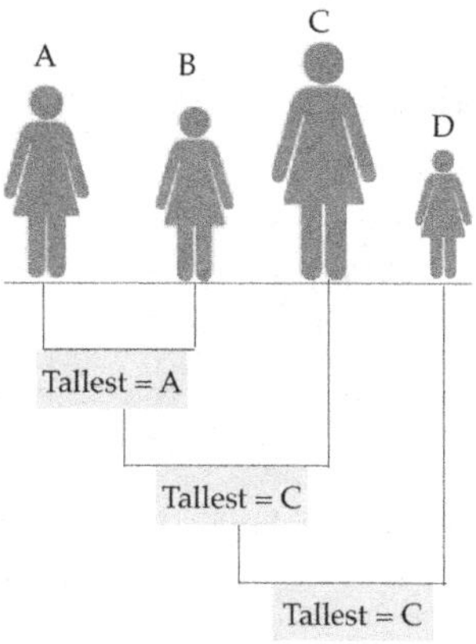

Figure 13: Example 1: Finding the tallest student in a class.

Example 2: Find the largest number in a sequence of numbers.

Solution: We can follow a similar procedure as in Example 1. Compare the first two numbers and then compare the larger among the two with the next number, and so on. See Figure 14 for an illustration where we compare four numbers, 5, 9, 1, and 11.

Example 3: Locate a student X (X stands for a name) on a list of students. Provide the position (index that starts from 0) of the student on the list.

Solution: We start from the first student and check if she is X. If yes, we return the index 0 as the answer and stop. If not, we compare X with the next student on the list. If success, return 1 as the index. Otherwise, perform the same task on the third, fourth, and later students. We stop this process as soon as X matches with an entry on the list. If X does not match with any student on the list, we report that X does not belong to the class. This process is called *searching*. In Figure 15 we illustrate how to locate X among the four students whose names are *Rohit, Sita, Ahilya,* and *Laxmi.*

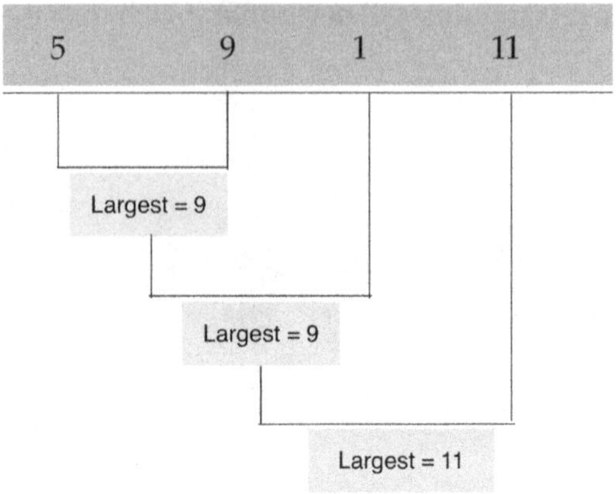

Figure 14: Example 2: Finding the largest number in a sequence of numbers.

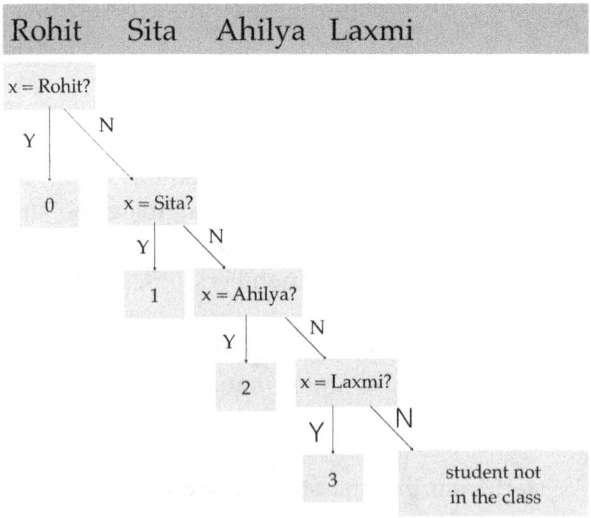

Figure 15: Example 3: Locating X on a list [Rohit, Sita, Ahilya, Laxmi]. Here, Y and N represent *yes* and *no* respectively.

Example 4: Mind-reading 1: A teacher thinks of a fruit in her head. Students have to figure out that fruit by asking questions to the teacher. A condition is that the teacher can only answer in yes and no.

Solution: Students can ask the teacher whether the fruit is banana. If yes, stop. If not, go to the next fruit—orange, grape, etc. Note that the present solution is similar to Example 3.

Example 5: Mind-reading 2: The teacher now thinks of a number between 1 to 8. Students have to figure out the number by asking questions to the teacher who will only answer in yes and no.

Solution: Students can figure out the desired number by following the steps outlined in Example 4. For example, ask if the number is 1, and then 2, etc. This algorithm is called *linear search*. See Figure 16 for an illustration.

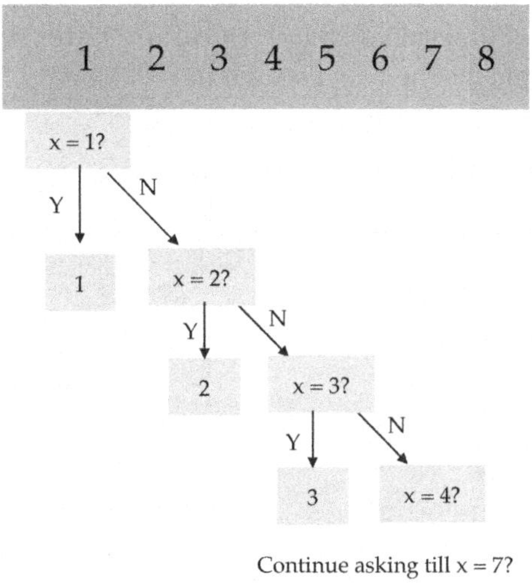

Figure 16: Example 5: Reading teacher's mind using linear search.

In the worst case scenario, the above solution requires 7 questions. However, we can solve the above problem using fewer queries using the following strategy. As an example, let us imagine that the teacher thinks of number 6. The student should ask the teacher the following set of questions:

Q1. Is the number less than equal to $8/2 = 4$?
A1: No.

Q2: Is the number less than or equal to 6?
A2: Yes.

Q3: Is the number 5?
A3: No.

The answer is 6.

In the above scheme, we keep bracketing the answer in the left half or the right half. This way, we can get to the answer using a maximum of 3 questions (not 7!). We can follow a similar scheme for other numbers as well, as shown in Figure 17. For example, for 3, we need to ask the questions, $x <= 4$?, $x<=2$?, $x=3$?

This search procedure, called *binary search*, works for sorted arrays. We follow similar logic for the word search in a dictionary.

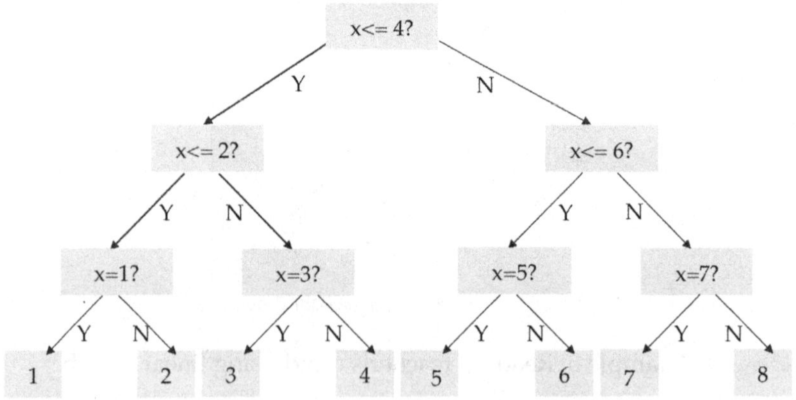

Figure 17: Example 5: Reading teacher's mind using binary search.

Example 6: Test whether a number n is prime number or not.

Solution: One of the factors of a non-prime number n is always less than equal to $\sqrt{n}$. For example, 21 has factor 3, which is less than $\sqrt{21}$. Therefore, we test if n is divisible by integers 2, 3, ..., $\sqrt{n}$. As soon as we find that n is divisible by any of these numbers, we can declare n to be a non-prime number. If n is indivisible by any of these numbers, then n is a prime number.

Many students perform the above test by going up to $n/2$. As stated above, we need not go all the way up to $n/2$.

The above problems involve definitive steps that can be performed by a computer. Hence, a computer can be programmed to solve these problems. Also, a computer can work with large numbers. For example, it can test if 9999999967 is a prime number or not, but most people, leaving out exceptions like Ramanujam, will dread to work on such problems. This is where computers have helped us immensely—solve problems involving large data sets.

We encourage the students to solve the exercises given at the end.

****

Conceptual questions

1. Some people argue that animals think like computers but some do not think that way. What is your view on this?

Exercises

1. Write an algorithm to compute the prime factors of a number. Example: The prime factors of 40 are 2,2,2,5.
2. Write an algorithm to compute the greatest common divisor (GCD) of two numbers.
3. Write an algorithm to compute the least common multiple (LCM) of two numbers
4. Compute all the prime numbers up to 100. State your algorithm.
5. Place 4 queens on a 4x4 chess board so that the queens do not kill each other. List all the solutions.
6. Place 8 queens on a 8x8 chess board so that the queens do not kill each other. List all the solutions.
7. A knight's tour: Construct a sequence of moves by a knight on

a chessboard such that the knight visits every square of the board exactly once. List all the solutions. Perform this task on a n x n chess board with $n = 3,4,5,6,7,8$.

8. We have 4 coins with one among them being heavier than the rest. Identify the defective coin using the least number of weighings on a traditional weighing balance (not digital ones!)? Find solutions for 8 coins and 12 coins as well. How will the solution change if the defective coin is lighter than the rest?

   Hint: For 4 coins, start with weighing coins 1 & 2 on one side and coins 2 & 3 on the other side of the weighing balance.

10. We have 4 coins among which one of them is defective (could be lighter or heavier). Identify the defective coin using the least number of weighings on a traditional weighing balance? Find solutions for 8 coins and 12 coins as well.

PART TWO

PROGRAMMING IN PYTHON

"Python is the most powerful language you can still read" —Paul Dubois

Chapter Three
INTEGERS IN COMPUTERS

Synopsis

"Numbers have life; they'r not just symbols on paper."
—Shakuntala Devi

"Integers are the fountainhead of all mathematics."
— Hermann Minkowski

Integers are used for counting—people, books, trees, etc. In this chapter we describe several number systems and computer representation of integers.

3.1 *Integers*

In modern representation of number system, a positive integer is represented as a sequence of digits. Here, the value of a digit in the number depends on its *place* or *position.* We can adopt any *base* for the number. In daily lives, we employ *decimal system* whose base is 10, while computer systems adopt *binary system* whose base is 2. We describe these number systems in the following discussion.

Decimal system

Decimal system, whose base is 10, has the following 10 digits: 0, 1, 2, 3, 4, 5, 6, 7, 8, 9. We illustrate the value of a number using an example:

$$(953)_{10} = 9\times10^2 + 5\times10^1 + 3\times10^0 = 9\times100 + 5\times10 + 3.$$

In 953, the digits 9, 5, and 3 have different weights: 9 multiplied by 100, 5 by 10, and 3 by 1. We present various components of the decimal number in Figure 18. The weights of a digit depend on its *position* or *index,* called *place value,* in the number. A digit with a higher index has more weight than that with a lower index. The subscript 10 of $(953)_{10}$ represents the *base* of the number.

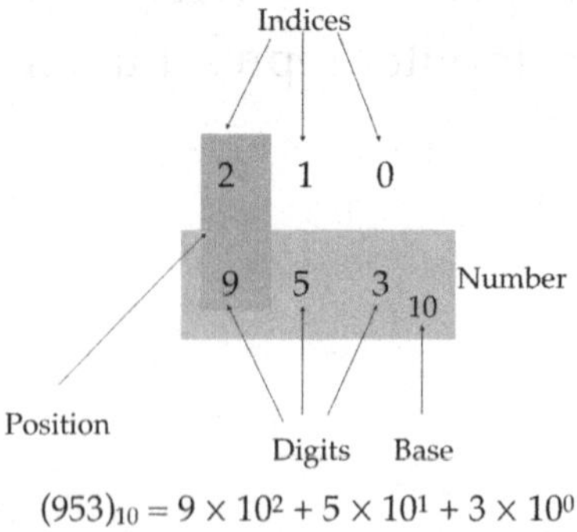

Figure 18: An example of a decimal number

A N-digit decimal integer is represented as $d_{n-1}\, d_{n-2}\, \ldots\, d_2\, d_1\, d_0$, and its value is

$$(d_n\, d_{n-1}\ \ldots\ d_0)_{10} = (d_n{\times}10^n + d_{n-1}{\times}10^{n-1} + \ldots + d_0\ ).$$

Here, $d_{n-1}, d_{n-2}, \ldots, d_1$, and d_0 are the digits of the number. The range of decimal number that can be generated with n digits is 0 to 10^n-1. For example, with 3 digits, we can represent numbers from 0 to 999 (10^3-1).

Binary system

Classical computers employ a binary system (base 2), whose digits are 0 and 1. The digits 0 and 1, called *bits,* represent spin-up and spin-down states of the magnetic memory unit of a computer (see Figure 19). Note that ON and OFF of a switch could also represent 1 and 0 bits.

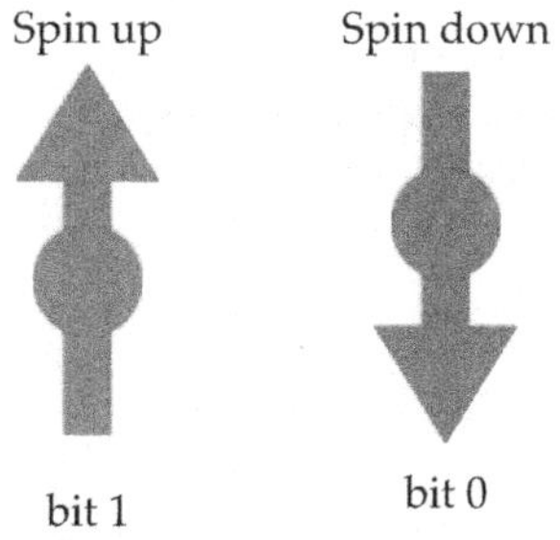

Figure 19: Illustration of spin-up and spin-down states that represent 1 and 0 bits respectively.

In Figure 20 we illustrate a binary number $(101)_2$, whose decimal value is 5:

$(101)_2 = 1{\times}2^2 + 0{\times}2^1 + 1{\times}2^0 = (5)_{10}$.

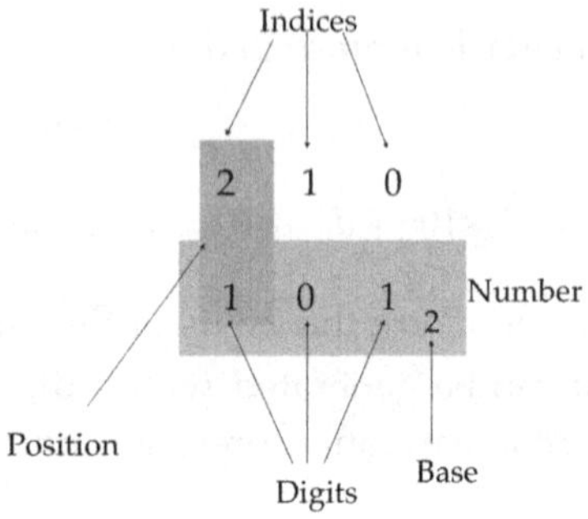

$(101)_2 = 1 \times 2^2 + 0 \times 2^1 + 1 \times 2^0 = (5)_{10}$

Figure 20: An example of a binary number

Some other examples binary numbers are

$(11)_2 = 1{\times}2^1 + 1{\times}2^0 = (3)_{10}$,
$(1101)_2 = 1{\times}2^3 + 1{\times}2^2 + 0{\times}2^1 + 1{\times}2^0 = (13)_{10}$.

A general binary number is represented as the following:

$$(b_n\, b_{n-1}\ \dots\ b_0\,)_2 = (b_n{\times}2^n + b_{n-1}{\times}2^{n-1} + \dots + b_0),$$

where b_i is the bit at the i-th index.

A *byte*, which is 8 bits, can represent the following set of positive numbers (with no sign bit):

$(0000\ 0000)_2 = 0$
$(0000\ 0001)_2 = (1)_{10}$
$(0000\ 0010)_2 = (1)_{10}$
....
$(1111\ 1111)_2 = (255)_{10}$

We provide the following table, which is useful for converting a binary number to its decimal equivalent.

2^0	2^1	2^2	2^3	2^4	2^5	2^6	2^7	2^8	2^9	2^{10}
1	2	4	8	16	32	64	128	256	512	1024

Example 1: Let us convert decimal number $(19)_{10}$ to binary. As shown in Figure 21(a), since $16 < 19 < 32$, we write $19 = 16 + 3$. Using $3 = 2 + 1$, we write $(19)_{10} = 16 + 2 + 1 = (10011)_2$. In this process, we proceed from top to bottom.

In Figure 21(b), we go from bottom to top. We divide 19 by 2 that yields 1 as a remainder. The quotient 9 is further divided by 2 that yields 4 and 1 as respective quotient and remainder. This process is continued till the quotient becomes 0. The remainders obtained in this process, 1,1,0,0,1, correspond to the coefficients of 2^0, 2^1, 2^2, 2^3, 2^4. Hence, $19 = (10011)_2$. Here, we start from b_0 and go up to b_4.

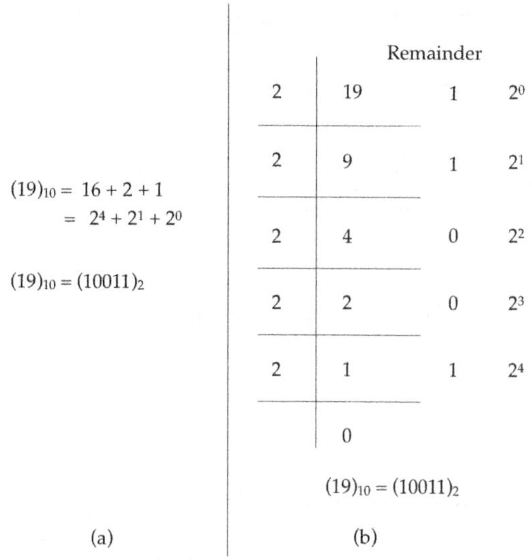

Figure 21: Conversion of $(19)_{10}$ to binary using two methods.

Using similar process as in Example 1, we deduce that

$$(251)_{10} = (11111011)_2$$
$$(181)_{10} = (10110101)_2$$

Octal and hexadecimal systems

Binary system requires many digits to represent large numbers. Therefore, for convenience, we convert decimal numbers to either *octal system* or *hexadecimal system,* whose bases are 8 and 16, respectively. The octal and hexadecimal numbers can be easily converted to binary numbers.

In octal system, the digits are 0, 1, 2, 3, 4, 5, 6, and 7. Here,

$$(s_{n-1}\, s_{n-2} \ldots s_2\, s_1\, s_0)_8 = s_{n-1}\times 8^{n-1} + s_{n-2}\times 8^{n-2} + \ldots$$
$$+ s_2\times 8^2 + s_1\times 8^1 + s_0\times 8^0,$$

where s_i's are the octal digits. An example of an octal number is

$$(11\ 111\ 011)_2 = (373)_8 = 3\times 8^2 + 7\times 8 + 3 = (251)_{10}.$$

In hexadecimal system, the digits are 0, 1, 2, …, 9, A, B, C, D, E, F. The digits A, B, C, D, E, F correspond to 10, 11, 12, 13, 14, 15 respectively. Here,

$$(h_{n-1}\, h_{n-2} \ldots h_2\, h_1\, h_0)_2 = h_{n-1}\times 16^{n-1} + h_{n-2}\times 16^{n-2} + \ldots$$
$$+ h_2\times 16^2 + h_1\times 16^1 + h_0\times 16^0.$$

The decimal number $(251)_{10}$ in hexadecimal is $(FB)_{16}$:

$$(1111\ 1011)_2 = (FB)_{16} = 15 \times 16 + 11 = (251)_{10}.$$

Note that for a conversion of a hexadecimal number to a binary number, we convert every hexadecimal digit to binary. For example, $(FB)_{16} = (1111\ 1011)_2$. A very similar scheme works for octal system. Clearly, the octal and hexadecimal numbers are more compact than their binary equivalents. The following tables are useful for converting decimal numbers to octal and hexadecimal systems.

	8^0	8^1	8^2	8^3	8^4
Decimal	1	8	64	512	4096

	16^0	16^1	16^2	16^3	16^4
Decimal	1	16	256	4096	65536

Example 2: Let us convert $(251)_{10}$ to octal system. Since $64 < 251 < 512$, we write $(251)_{10} = 3x64 + 59$. Using $59 = 7x8 + 3$, we deduce that $(251)_{10} = (373)_8$.

In this section, we covered decimal, binary, octal, and hexadecimal representations of integers. Note, however, that we could have other number systems as well. For example, we can construct number systems with bases 3, 5, and 9. It is not clear why decimal system has become a norm for our daily lives; some believe that it may have arisen due to counting using ten fingers. Also note that a number is unique, but its representations vary in different number systems.

****

Conceptual questions

1. Why do we employ a binary system for computers?
2. Why is the decimal system more suited for daily lives than the binary system?

Exercises

1. Convert the following binary numbers to decimal numbers:
   (a) 101 (b) 11001 (c) 1001001 (d) 11111111 (e) 11100111
2. Convert the following decimal numbers to binary numbers:
   (a) 10 (b) 16 (c) 95 (d) 254 (e) 555
3. Convert the following decimal numbers to octal numbers:
   (a) 10 (b) 16 (c) 95 (d) 254 (e) 555

4. Convert the following decimal numbers to hexadecimal numbers:

   (a) 10 (b) 16 (c) 95 (d) 254 (e) 555

5. Convert the following octal numbers to decimal and binary numbers:

   (a) 11 (b) 17 (c) 75 (d) 254 (e) 545

6. Convert the following hexadecimal numbers to decimal and binary numbers:

   (a) 1F (b) DD (c) 7F (d) F54 (e) 555

3.2 Integers in Python

In this section we will describe integer representation and integer operations in Python.

A byte, which is 8 bits, can hold only 2^8 or 256 different integers (for example, −128 to 127). The number 127, however, is too small for any practical application (for example, counting population). Therefore, computers typically employ 4 bytes or 8 bytes to store integers. However, in Python, an integer can be of any length. If needed, Python uses more than 8 bytes to store long integers.

With 32 bits or 4 bytes, the first bit is reserved for the sign of the number: 0 for positive integers and 1 for negative integers. Hence, the range of integers represented by 4 bytes is -2^{31} to $2^{31}-1$, or −2147483648 to 2147483647. Considering that

$$2^{10} = 1024 \approx 10^3,$$

we estimate 2^{31} as $2 \times (10^3)^3$ or $2x10^9$.

The addition, subtraction, multiplication, and integer division operators in Python are +, −, *, and // respectively. The power operator in Python is **, hence, we represent a^b as a**b. Some examples of the above operators are

```
In [1]: 45+95
Out[1]: 140

In [2]: 45-95
Out[2]: -50

In [3]: 45*95
Out[3]: 4275

In [4]: 45//95
Out[4]: 0

In [5]: 95//45
Out[5]: 2

In [6]: 2**3
Out[6]: 8
```

In the above statements, *In* [] contains an input to the Python interpreter, while *Out* [] contains the output by the interpreter. Note that Python interprets the above integers as decimal numbers. Also, the integer division operator, //, differs from real-division operator, / (to be discussed in the next chapter). For example,

```
In [7]: 95/45
Out[7]: 2.111111111111111
```

Another useful integer operator is *modulus* that yields the remainder of an integer division. In Python, the remainder operator is %. For example,

```
In [8]: 50%3
Out[8]: 2
```

We often encounter integer expressions with more than one operators. Under such situations, we follow the precedence rules given in Table 1.

Table 1: Precedences of arithmetic operators involving integers.

Operator	Function
** (Highest precedence)	Power
*,//,%	Multiplication, Integer division, Modulus
+,- (Lowest precedence)	Add, Subtract

Note that

1. Operators with the highest precedence are evaluated first.
2. *, //, % have same precedence.
3. + and – have same precedence.
4. In case of multiple operators with same precedence, they are evaluated from left to right.
5. Brackets are used to override precedence.

We illustrate these rules using the following examples:

```
In [9]: 2+3//2
Out[9]: 3

In [10]: (2+3)//2
```

```
Out[10]: 2

In [11]: 16//4//2
Out[11]: 2

In [12]: 16//(4//2)
Out[12]: 8
```

In the line *In* [9], 3//2 = 1 is evaluated first due to higher precedence of // over +. After this, the result is added to 2. However, if we need to evaluate the addition operation first, then the addition operation must be enclosed within brackets (see *In* [10]). In the expression of *In* [11], following the second rule given above, 16//4 is evaluated first, after which the result is divided by 2. In the next example, 16//(4//2), (4/2) is evaluated first due to the brackets.

Python also provides functions for computing the binary, octal, and hex equivalents of a given integer. In the following examples, we convert a decimal number $(100)_{10}$ to binary, octal, and hex numbers.

```
In [18]: x= 100

In [21]: bin(x)
Out[21]: '0b1100100'

In [22]: oct(x)
Out[22]: '0o144'

In [23]: hex(x)
Out[23]: '0x64'

In [24]: hex(2147483647)
Out[24]: '0x7fffffff'
```

In the above code segment, 0b, 0o, and 0x represent respectively the binary, octal, and hex representations. We can also convert a number in any number representation (given as a string) to its decimal equivalent using the *int* operator.

```
In [86]: int('1110',2) # '1110' in base 2
Out[86]: 14

In [87]: int('1110',10) # '1110' in base 10
Out[87]: 1110
```

```
In [88]: int('111F',16) # '1110' in base 16
Out[88]: 4383

In [89]: int('1110',3)  # '1110' in base 3
Out[89]: 39
```

The strings after # represent comments, which are not evaluated by Python. Note that the function *int* gives decimal number as output.

Computers represent numbers using the binary system. Therefore, the sizes of memory devices are 2^n, where n is an integer. For example, a byte has $2^3 = 8$ bits. The size of RAM is typically given in gigabytes (GB). For example, it could be

4 GB = 4×2^{30} bytes.

Note that $2^{10} = 1024 \approx 10^3$. Therefore, 4 GB = $4 \times (2^{10})^3 \approx 4 \times 10^9$. Other computer lingo are

1 Kilobyte = 1 KB = $2^{10} \approx 10^3$
1 Megabyte = 1 MB = $2^{20} \approx 10^6$
1 Terabyte = 1 TB = $2^{40} \approx 10^{12}$
1 Petabyte = 1 PB = $2^{50} \approx 10^{15}$
1 Exabyte = 1 EB = $2^{60} \approx 10^{18}$

The RAM of a calculator is around 4 to 8 KB, while that of a mobile is around 1 GB. Supercomputers have much larger RAM (in petabytes).

RAM storage is volatile. That is, its contents disappear when the computer is switched off. We use a hard disk for permanent storage. A typical hard disk of a personal computer has a capacity of terabytes, while those of supercomputers go from petabytes to exabytes. Mobiles have hard disk storage in the range of 64 GB to 128 GB.

****

Exercises

1. Evaluate the following integer expressions in Python and state your results:
   - 3**3, 9//2, 9/2, 4–6–3, 4–(6–3), 10+90//7, 4//3*7, 4*7//3, 9*2**3
2. Gayatri's laptop has 8 GB RAM. What is the RAM size in decimal representation? How many integers (assuming 8 byte integers) can be stored in this RAM?
3. In the previous section, you converted several decimal numbers to binary and vice versa. Test these conversions using Python functions *bin*(), *oct*(), *hex*(), and *int*().

CHAPTER FOUR
REAL NUMBERS IN COMPUTERS

Synopsis

"Although he may not always recognize his bondage, modern man lives under a tyranny of numbers."
— Nicholas Eberstadt

Real numbers represent quantities that vary continuously, for example, time, distance, and velocity. In this chapter we explore how Python helps us work with real numbers.

4.1 Real Numbers

In daily lives, we encounter real numbers all the time, e.g., vehicle speed, distance travelled, weights, etc. In mathematics, we represent a real number using *fraction notation* and *decimal-point notation.* For example, half is represented as ½, which is a fraction, or as 0.5, which is in decimal-point notation. However, in computers, the real numbers are represented using decimal-point notation (not as fractions). An important point to remember is that in Python, real numbers are also called *float,* a short form for *floating point number,* which will be described later in this section.

A real number can be rational or irrational. Irrational numbers (for example, √2, π, and *e*) require an infinite number of digits in decimal point notation. Some rational numbers too require infinite number of digits for their representation. For example, in point notation, ⅓ requires an infinite number of decimal digits (0.3333…). However, ½, which is 0.5, requires only one nonzero digit in decimal-point notation.

First we describe the decimal system of real numbers.

Decimal system

Often, we represent a real number as

$$(d_n\, d_{n-1}\ \ldots\ d_0.\, d_{-1}\ \ldots\ d_{-m}\,)_{10} = (d_n\times 10^n + d_{n-1}\times 10^{n-1}+\ldots$$
$$+\, d_0 + d_{-1}\times 10^{-1} + \ldots + d_{-m}\times 10^{-m}).$$

In the above decimal number, the number of digits is n+m+1. A specific example is

$$(32.54)_{10} = 3\text{x}10 + 2\text{x}1 + 5\text{x}10^{-1} + 4\text{x}10^{-2}$$

which is illustrated in Figure 22. The number to the left of the decimal point is called *integer,* while that to the right of the decimal point is called *fraction.* The point separating the integer and fraction is called the *decimal point.* Clearly, the weights of the digits decrease as we go from left to right. In $(32.54)_{10}$, 5 has a weight of one-tenth, while 4 has weight of one-hundredth. As described in the last chapter, 3 and 2 have weights of 10 and 1 respectively. The above number is also written as 0.3254×10^2, or as 0.3254E2; this representation is called *exponential notation.*

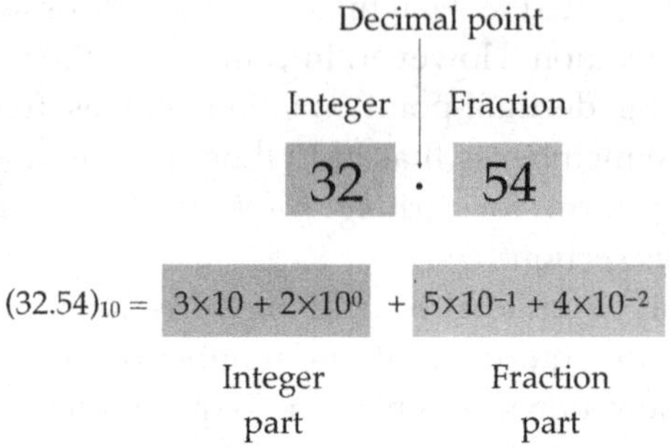

Figure 22: A decimal number $(32.54)_{10}$

Binary system

A binary number is

$$(b_n\, b_{n-1}\, \ldots\, b_0.\, b_{-1}\, \ldots\, b_{-m})_{10} = (b_n \times 2^n + b_{n-1} \times 2^{n-1} + \ldots + b_0 + b_{-1} \times 2^{-1} + \ldots + b_{-m} \times 2^{-m}).$$

Examples of binary numbers are 1.1, 1.01, 1011.101, 1.011101×2^3. In binary representation, after the dot, the weights decrease as one-half, one-quarter, one-eighth, and so on. Note that the number 1.011101×2^3 or 1.011101E3 (in exponential notation) is equal to 1011.101.

Following the definition of binary representation, we can easily convert a binary number to its decimal equivalent. For example,

$$(11.101)_2 = 2^1 + 2^0 + 2^{-1} + 2^{-3} = 2 + 1 + 0.5 + 0.125 = (3.625)_{10},$$

which is illustrated in Figure 23. Here, similar to the decimal system, the number to the left of the middle point is called *integer*, while that to the right of the point is called *fraction*. The middle point, called *binary point*, separates the integer and fraction.

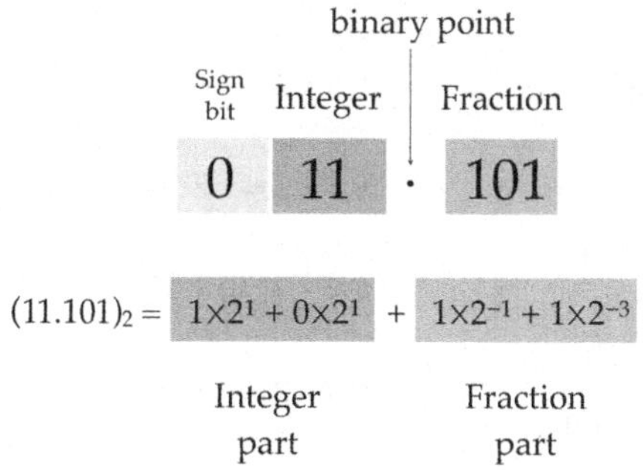

Figure 23: A binary number $(11.101)_2$

The integer part of a decimal number (e.g., 32 of 32.54) is converted to binary as described in the previous chapter (see Figure 21). The fraction is converted to binary representation by repeated multiplication with 2, as illustrated in the following examples.

Example 1: We convert decimal numbers 0.375 to binary. See Figure 24(a) for all the steps. First, we multiply 0.375 by 2 and collect the whole number (0) as the first binary digit after the binary point. The new fraction, 0.75, is multiplied again by 2 and the resulting whole number, 1, is collected as the second binary digit. We continue this process until fraction = 0. This process yields $(0.375)_{10} = (0.011)_2$. We can verify the correctness of the conversion process: $1/4 + 1/8 = 0.375$. Note that 0.375 requires a finite number of digits in both decimal and binary representations.

Example 2: We convert decimal numbers 0.8 to binary. As shown in Figure 24(b), 0.8→1.6→0.6→1.2→0.2→0.4→0.8. Note that 0.8 recurs after 4 steps. Therefore, $(0.8)_{10} = (0.1100\ 1100\ 1100\ \ldots\ )_2$ with a recurrence of 1100. Thus, the conversion process from decimal to binary does not converge for this number. Note that $(0.8)_{10}$ has a finite number of digits in the decimal system, but its representation in the binary system requires an infinite number of bits.

	frac	integer	
0.375 x 2 = 0.75	0.75	0	b_{-1}
0.75 x 2 = 1.5	0.5	1	b_{-2}
0.5 x 2 = 1	0	1	b_{-3}

$(0.375)_{10} = (0.011)_2$

(a)

	frac	integer	
0.8 x 2 = 1.6	0.6	1	b_{-1}
0.6 x 2 = 1.2	0.2	1	b_{-2}
0.2 x 2 = 0.4	0.4	0	b_{-3}
0.4 x 2 = 0.8	0.8	0	b_{-4}

$(0.8)_{10} = (0.11001100\ldots)_2$

(b)

Figure 24: Conversion of decimal numbers to binary numbers: (a) 0.375, (b) 0.8.

Example 3: $(⅓)_{10} = (0.01\ 01\ 01\ \ldots)_2$ with a recurrence of 01. Note that $(⅓)_{10} = (0.3333\ \ldots)_{10}$. Thus, both decimal and binary representations of $(⅓)_{10}$ require an infinite number of digits. However, $(⅓)_{10}$ requires only one digit in tertiary (base 3) system: $(⅓)_{10} = (0.1)_3$.

More examples:

$(1.1)_{10} = (1.0001\ 1001\ 1001\ 1001\ \ldots\ )_2$ with a recurrence of 1001
$(1.5)_{10} = 1+1/2 = (1.1)_2$
$(15.0)_{10} = 8+4+2+1 = (1111)_2 = 1.111\text{x}2^3$
$(150.0)_{10} = 9\text{x}16+6 = (1001\ 0110)_2 = 1.001\ 0110\text{x}2^7$
$(1.75)_{10} = 1+1\text{x}2^{-1} + 2^{-2} = (1.11)_2$

A computer has a finite number of digits. Hence, even in principle, some numbers like ⅓, $(0.8)_{10}$, and √2 cannot be represented accurately in a computer.

Hexadecimal system

A hexadecimal number is

$$(h_n\, h_{n-1}\, \ldots\, h_0.\, h_{-1}\, \ldots\, h_{-m}\,)_x = (h_n{\times}16^n + h_{n-1}{\times}16^{n-1} + \ldots$$
$$+\, h_0 + h_{-1}{\times}16^{-1} + \ldots + h_{-m}{\times}16^{-m}).$$

Examples:

$(0.CC)_x = 12/16 + 12/162 = (0.796875)_{10}$
$(1.A)_x = 1{+}10/16 = (1.625)_{10}$

We convert a decimal number to hexadecimal number by following the same procedure as that followed for decimal to binary conversion.

Example 4: We convert $(0.375)_{10}$ to hexadecimal number by multiplying the fraction with 16. The procedure is very similar to that shown in Figure 24. We multiply 0.375 with 16 that yields $(12)_{10}$ or C_x, which is h_{-1}. We stop at this stage because the fraction is zero. Hence, $(0.375)_{10} = (0.C)_x$.

Example 5: We convert $(0.8)_{10}$ to a hexadecimal number. The multiplication operation, 0.8x16, yields 12 as the whole number and 0.8 as the fraction. We obtain the same result for the next iteration. Hence, $(0.8)_{10} = (0.CC\ \ldots)_x$; the iteration does not terminate for $(0.8)_{10}$.

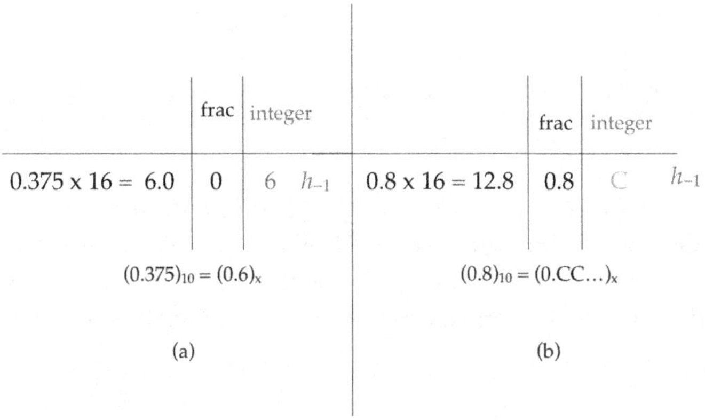

Figure 25: Conversion of a decimal numbers to hexadecimal numbers: (a) 0.375, (b) 0.8.

Following similar arguments as in Examples 4 and 5, we obtain the following results.

$(⅓)_{10} = (0.55\ldots)_x$ with a recurrence of 5
$(1.1)_{10} = (1.1999\ldots)_x$ with a recurrence of 9
$(1.5)_{10} = (1.8)_x$
$(1.75)_{10} = (1.C)_x$

Representations of real numbers in computers

In computers, real numbers are stored using floating point representation in which the binary point floats (moves) depending on the exponent. For example, $(1111)_2$ is stored as $1.111 x 2^3$ in the computer, while $(0.011)_2$ is stored as $1.1 x\ 2^{-2}$. The integer part is always 1.

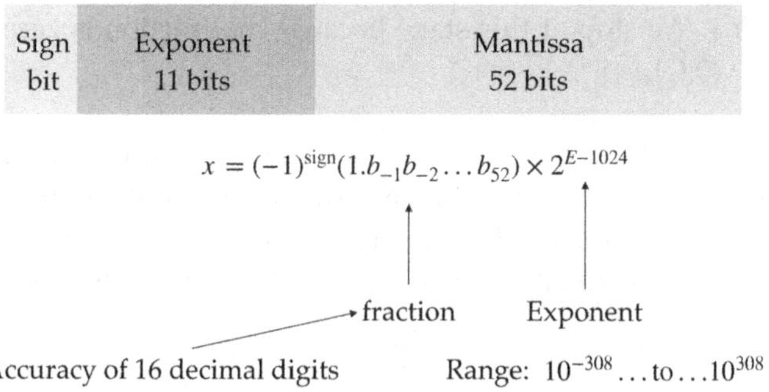

Figure 26: Representation of a real number inside a computer using 64 bits.

At present, it is a standard practice to use 64 bits to store a real number in a computer. Among the 64 bits, 52 bits are reserved for the fraction, 11 bits for the exponent, and 1 bit for the sign. See Figure 26 for an illustration. We state without proof that the above arrangement leads to an accuracy of 16 decimal digits and range of numbers from 10^{-308} to 10^{308}. For example, 1/3 is stored as 0.3333 3333 3333 3333, with the other digits ignored. The largest number that can be stored in the above representation is

$f_{max} = (1.7976931348623157)_{10} \times 10^{308}$.

In the next section, we will present how to work with real numbers in Python.

****

Conceptual questions

1. Why do we need real numbers when we already have integers?
2. Computers employ a finite number of bits to store real numbers. What is the consequence of this feature on the accuracy of the real numbers.

Exercises

1. Convert the following decimal numbers to exponential notation with the first digit after the decimal point as the first nonzero digit (for example, 0.3254E2):
   7890.45, 0.0189, 30179890
2. Convert the following binary numbers to exponential notation with 1 as the only bit before the binary point (for example, 1.01E4):
   0.0010011, 0.11101, 111111.101
3. Convert the following binary numbers to decimal numbers:
   (a) 1.01 (b) 11.1 (c) 0.1001 (d) 1111.11 (e) 11.101
4. Convert the following decimal numbers to binary numbers:
   (a) 1/8 (b) 1/10 (c) 14.0 (d) 7/10 (e) 256.0
5. Convert the following hexadecimal numbers to decimal numbers:
   (a) 0.F (b) F.F (c) 1.8 (d) 0.C (e) 0.A
6. Convert the following decimal numbers to hexadecimal numbers:
   (a) 1.6 (b) 1.4 (c) 0.9 (d) 1/3 (e) 0.256
7. Convert the following octal numbers to decimal numbers:

(a) 0.7 (b) 1.6 (c) 7.1 (d) 2.5 (e) 1.2

8. Convert the following decimal numbers to octal numbers:
(a) 1/4 (b) 1/10 (c) 1.4 (d) 1/8 (e) 0.256

4.2 Real Numbers in Python

As described in the previous section, the real numbers are typically stored in a computer using 64 bits: 52 bits for the fraction, 11 bits for the exponent, and 1 bit for the sign. See Figure 26 for an illustration.

For real numbers, the operators for addition, subtraction, multiplication, and division are +, −, *, and / respectively. The power function a^b is implemented as *a****b*. Examples of these operators are

```
In [1]: 1+2.5
Out[1]: 3.5

In [2]: 1-2.5
Out[2]: -1.5

In [3]: 2*3.5
Out[3]: 7.0

In [4]: 2/3.5
Out[4]: 0.5714285714285714

In [5]: 2.5**3
Out[5]: 15.625
```

If any of the two arguments of the above operators is real, then the result is converted to a real number.

Table 2: Precedences of arithmetic operators involving real numbers

Operator	Function
** (Highest precedence)	Power
*,/	Multiplication, Division
+,- (Lowest precedence)	Add, Subtract

Often, we have expressions with multiple operators. In such cases, the expressions are computed using the precedence rules given in Table 2. Note that

1. Operators with the highest precedence are evaluated first.
2. * and / have the same precedence, so do + and −.
3. In case of multiple operators with the same precedence, the

operators are evaluated from left to right.

4. Brackets are used to override precedence.

These rules are illustrated using the following examples.

```
In [6]: 2.5+3/2
Out[6]: 4.0

In [7]: (2.5+3)/2
Out[7]: 2.75

In [8]: 3/2/4
Out[8]: 0.375

In [9]: 3/(2/4)
Out[9]: 6.0
```

In the expression of *In* [6], 3/2 is evaluated first due to higher precedence of / over +. After this, the result, 1.5, is added to 2.5. If we want to evaluate the addition first, then the expression must be enclosed within brackets (see *In* [7]). In the expression of *In* [8], following the second rule, 3/2 is evaluated first, after which the result is divided by 4. In the next example, (2/4) is evaluated first due to the brackets.

Important constants such as π, e are already stored in Python.

```
In [10]: e
Out[10]: 2.718281828459045

In [11]: pi
Out[11]: 3.141592653589793
```

There are many function involving real numbers, for example, *log*(), *sin*(), *cos*(), *exp*(). All these functions take a real number as an argument. Refer to the illustrations given below.

```
In [12]: log(2)
Out[12]: 0.6931471805599453

In [13]: log2(4)
Out[13]: 2.0

In [14]: log10(100)
```

```
Out[14]: 2.0

In [15]: sin(pi/2)
Out[15]: 1.0

In [16]: cos(pi/4)
Out[16]: 0.7071067811865476

In [17]: exp(3)
Out[17]: 20.085536923187668

In [18]: sqrt(2)
Out[18]: 1.4142135623730951
```

Note that *log, log2,* and *log10* are logarithms with the bases e, 2, and 10 respectively. Some other useful functions for real numbers are *int*() and *round*(). The function *int* truncates a real number and gives a whole number, while the function *round* rounds up the real number to the nearest integer.

```
In [19]: int(13.5)
Out[19]: 13

In [20]: round(13.6)
Out[20]: 14

In [21]: round(13.1)
Out[21]: 13

In [22]: round(13.5)
Out[22]: 14
```

Note that the real numbers are often truncated. The error occurring due to the truncation of the real numbers is called *truncation error.*

Example:

```
In [27]: 1/3
Out[27]: 0.3333333333333333

In [28]: 1.1*3
Out[28]: 3.3000000000000003

In [29]: 1.1*3-3.3
Out[29]: 4.440892098500626e-16
```

```
In [30]: 1.5*3
Out[30]: 4.5

In [31]: 1.5*3-4.5
Out[31]: 0.0
```

Computer-generated 3*1.1 does not match with the exact value of 3.3. This is because 1.1 is not represented exactly in the binary system. The truncation error for 1.5 is zero because 1.5 is represented exactly in the computer. Refer to the previous section for the representations of 1.1 and 1.5.

The hex representation of a decimal number can be computed in Python using the function *float.hex*(). For example,

```
In [25]: float.hex(1.0/3)
Out[25]: '0x1.5555555555555p-2'

In [26]: float.hex(1.1)
Out[26]: '0x1.199999999999ap+0'

In [27]: float.hex(1.5)
Out[27]: '0x1.8000000000000p+0'

In [28]: float.hex(1.75)
Out[28]: '0x1.c000000000000p+0'
```

In the outputs of the above Python statements (*Out* []), 0x represents the hex representation, while $p+n$ at the end represents 2^n, where n is an integer. These results are consistent with the results discussed in the previous section. Note that

$$(⅓)_{10} = (0.01\ 01\ 01\ \ldots)_2 = (1.0101\ 0101\ \ldots)_2 \times 2^{-2} = (1.55\ \ldots)_x \times 2^{-2}.$$

We end this section with a remark that in some computers, real numbers are stored using 16 bits or 32 bits. Such computers are called 16-bit or 32-bit machines respectively. We employ such schemes when computational accuracy is not critical, for example, for storing and manipulating images in Graphical Processor Units (GPU). Note that in a 32-bit machine, the largest real number that can be stored is

$$f_{\max} = (3.4028235)_{10} \times 10^{38}.$$

Thus, the accuracy of a 32-bit machine is 8 digits.

****

Exercises

1. Evaluate the following expressions:
   - 2//3*4.0, 2/3*4.0, 3.0-4*5/3, 3*4/5/6, 3*4/(5/6), 2**3*4, 2**0.5
2. Evaluate the following expressions in Python:
   - Sin(pi/4), exp(1), log(1), log(2), log10(2), log2(2), int(1.3), int(1.7), int(10.5), round(99.5), round(90.8), sqrt(3)
3. Compute the expressions, 0.5*7, 0.8*7, 0.7*3, in Python. Explain the discrepancies if any.
4. In Exercises of Section 4.1, you converted several decimal numbers to binary and hex number systems. Verify these conversions using Python function *float.hex*().

CHAPTER FIVE

VARIABLES AND LOGIC IN PYTHON

Synopsis

"We are living in a computer-programmed reality, and the only clue we have to it is when some variable is changed, and some alteration in reality occurs. We have the overwhelming impression that we were reliving the present - deja vu."

— Philip K. Dick

In this chapter we will discuss Python variables as well as logical variables.

5.1 Python Variables & Logical Variables

It is time to discuss *Python variables*. In Python, a variable is a name associated with data. For example, in the following Python statement, variable x represents 10.

```
In [1]: x=10
```

In the above statement, $x = 10$ does not mean equality. Instead, the above statement implies that x is associated with object 8 ($x \longleftrightarrow 8$). Here, = is an assignment operator. We can get the value of x by typing x:

```
In [2]: x
Out[2]: 10
```

An operation on x is equivalent to an operation on its associated object, which is 10. For example,

```
In [3]: x**3
Out[3]: 1000
```

We can print x or any expression involving x using the *print* function. For example,

```
In [4]: print(x, x**3)
10   1000
```

We can use an existing Python variable to assign to other data. For example, we can reassign x to another number, say 5.5, as shown below:

```
In [5]: x = 5.5

In [6]: x
Out[6]: 5.5
```

Now, x is associated with the new number 5.5, which is a real number, not an integer. In later chapters, we show that Python variables can refer to characters, strings, and arrays.

We remark that several Python statements can be written in a single line as long as they are separated by semicolons. For example,

```
In [47]: x=5; y = 6; z = x*y; print("x = ", x, "y =", y, "z = ",  z)
  x =  5 y = 6 z =  30
```

In the print statement, "x =", "y = ", and "z =" are strings that are printed as is.

Variable names and Keywords

According to Python syntax, Python variable names can be of any length. However, the names of Python variables should follow the following norms:

1. A variable name must start with a letter or the underscore character (_).
2. A variable name cannot start with a number.
3. A variable name can contain alpha-numeric characters (A-Z, a-z, 0-9) and underscore (_). It cannot contain any other character including special characters, such as $,%, etc.
4. Variable names are case-sensitive. For example, *a* and *A* are different variables, so are India and india.

Example 1: Examples of valid Python variable names are *temp, sum, total, weight, year_beyond_2000, _partial_sum*. However, *3sons, man%power, man power, total$* are invalid names for Python variables.

While writing programs, it is best to choose proper names for the variables. It is easy to decipher and understand a program with such choices. For example, for the city temperature, *temperature* is a good choice for the variable name, while *temp* or *t* are not.

Note however that some reserved words, called *keywords*, can not be used as Python variables. Here is the list of Python keywords:

and, as, assert, break, class, continue, def, del, elif, else, except, False, finally, for, from, global, if, import, in, ls, lambda, none, nonlocal, not, or, pass, raise, return, True, try, while, with, yield

The above words have special meaning. For example, *True* is one of the boolean values. Consequently, keywords cannot be used as variable names.

Example 2: An assignment *In* [68]: *True* = *3* yields an error "SyntaxError: can't assign to keyword".

Logical Variables in Python

Logic plays a significant role in computer programming. In this section, we will briefly describe *logical variables* and *logical expressions* in Python. George Boole first formulated the mathematics of logic. In his honour, logical variables are also called *Boolean variables.*

Logical data type takes a value, *True* or *False.* A logical expression also takes one of these two values. Examples of logical expressions are

```
In [28]: 5 < 6
Out[28]: True

In [29]: 5 > 6
Out[29]: False
```

The statement of *In* [28] "5 < 6" is read as "Is 5 less than 6?". This is true, hence the logical expression yields *True* as output. The next statement refers to "Is 5 greater than 6?", which is *False.*

We check the equality of two expressions using the equality operator ==. For examples,

```
In [33]: 5 == 6
Out[33]: False

In [34]: 5 == 5
Out[34]: True
```

The statement of *In* [33] "5 == 6" is interpreted as "Is 5 equal to 6?".

Hence 5 == 6 is *False*. In addition, *comparison operators* <=, >=, != stand for "less than equal to", "greater than equal to", and "not equal to", respectively. The meaning of these operators is obvious. A comprehensive list of comparative operators is given in Table 3.

Table 3: A list of comparative operators

Operator	Name	Example
==	Equal	x == y
!=	Not equal	x != y
>	Greater than	x>y
<	Less than	x<y
>=	Greater than or equal to	x>= y
<=	Less than or equal to	x<=y

We can combine logical expressions using boolean operators *and, or, xor,* and *not,* as illustrated below. We start with *or* operator.

```
In [38]: is_summer = (month == 5) or (month == 6) or
(month == 7)

In [40]: month = 5

In [41]: is_summer
Out[41]: True
```

According to the statement of *In* [38], *is_summer* is a logical variable that takes a value *True* when the *month* is May (5th month) or June (6th month) or July (7th month); it is *False* otherwise. After this, we illustrate the *and* operator.

```
In [7]: angles_equal = True

In [8]: sides_equal = True

In [9]: is_square = (angles_equal == True) and
(sides_equal == True)

In [10]: is_square
Out[10]: True

In [11]: sides_equal = False
```

```
In [13]: is_square = (angles_equal == True) and
(sides_equal == True)

In [14]: is_square
Out[14]: False
```

A quadrangle is a square if and only if all the sides and the angles of the quadrangle are equal. The boolean variable *is_square* is True when both the conditions are True. The variable *is_square* is false when either of the two conditions is false. The above example illustrates the operator *and*.

After this, we illustrate the *not* operator. A person is well if she is not sick. Hence is_well = not(is_sick).

```
In [16]: is_sick = True

In [17]: is_well = not(is_sick)

In [18]: is_well
Out[18]: False
```

For two boolean variables *A* and *B*, the Truth table of Table 4 lists the results of *or, and,* and *not* operations with *A* and *B*. For example, in the first row, the variables *A* and *B* are both *True*. With these values, the results are as follow: *True and True = True; True or True = True; not True = False*. In the table, we also list the results of the *exclusive-or* (*xor*) operator. *A xor B* is true if either of the two operands, but not both, is True. Note that the *xor* operator is not available in Python.

Table 4: Truth table (*T = True* and *F = False*)

A	*B*	*A and B*	*A or B*	*A xor B*	*not A*
T	*T*	*T*	*T*	*F*	*F*
T	*F*	*F*	*T*	*T*	*F*
F	*T*	*F*	*T*	*T*	*T*
F	*F*	*F*	*F*	*F*	*T*

In case of multiple boolean operators, the sequence of operations is decided by the precedence of operators, which is listed in Table 5.

Table 5: Precedences of logical operators (from highest to lowest)

Operator	Function
<, <=, >, >=, !=, == (highest)	Comparison
not	Boolean NOT
and	Boolean AND
or	Boolean OR

Some more examples of boolean operations are given below.

```
In [96]: P = True

In [97]: Q = False

In [98]: P and Q
Out[98]: False

In [99]: P or Q
Out[99]: True

In [100]: not P
Out[100]: False
```

Another interesting feature of Python is that the boolean values of strings, and nonzero integers and floats are *True*, while those of 0, 0.0, and '' (empty string) are *False*. See the illustration below.

```
In [108]: bool(5), bool(-5.0), bool('c')
Out[108]: (True, True, True)

In [112]: bool(0), bool(0.0), bool('')
Out[112]: (False, False, False)
```

With this we end our discussion on Python variables.

****

Conceptual questions

1. What are the differences between = and == operators of Python?

Exercises

1. Given three logical variables, *A = True, B=True, and C=False,* evaluate the following logical expressions:
    - A and C, A or C, not C, A and B and C, A and B or C, not A or B or C, bool(10.0), bool(0).
2. Suppose $x = 5$ and $y = 10$. What are the outputs of the following logical expressions?
    - $x < y$, $x <= y$, $x == y$, $x != y$, $x < $ y or x > y, x<y, x >y

CHAPTER SIX

STRINGS, LISTS, AND ARRAYS IN PYTHON

Synopsis

"Words and Ideas can change the world"
— Dead Poet Society (movie)

In this chapter, we describe strings, list, and Numpy arrays.

6.1 Characters and Strings

Character is an important data type of Python. Alphabets and digits are characters. In Python, a character is enclosed within single quotes (') or double quotes ("); both these quotes are used interchangeably. Examples of characters are `S', 'C', "9".

```
In [1]: 'S'
Out[1]: 'S'

In [2]: "9"
Out[2]: '9'
```

A character is typically stored using 1 byte. However, some multilingual characters, such as अ of Hindi, require more than 1 byte.

A set of characters form a string. For example,

```
In [7]: x = "This is a string."

In [8]: x
Out[8]: 'This is a string.'
```

In the statement of *In* [7], *x* is a variable that refers to a string. In the above example, blank (' ' with a single space) is also a character.

Plus (+) is a *concatenation* operator that adds two strings. Multiplication of a string by an integer *m* yields a larger string containing *m* copies of that string; this is called a *replication* operation. Note that we cannot add a string to an integer. For example, 3+'9' is an invalid operation; Python will report an error for this statement. We illustrate the above operations using the following examples:

```
In [70]: 'SS'+'T'
Out[70]: 'SST'

In [71]: 5*'S'
Out[71]: 'SSSSS'

In [74]: x + "  Hi, string"
Out[74]: 'This is a string.  Hi, string'
```

To continue a string to the next line, we use the backslash character

('\') for a line break.

```
In [77]: 'I am going to the center of the \
    ...: Earth'

Out[77]: 'I am going to the center of the Earth'
```

We can read a string from a keyboard using the function input().

```
In [24]: x= input("Enter the value of x =")
Enter the value of x =10

In [25]: x
Out[25]: '10'
```

Note that *input*() returns a string. Hence, in the above statement, x, which is '10', is a string, not an integer. To convert *x* to an integer, we need the following Python statement.

```
In [24]: x = int(input("Enter the value of x ="))
Enter the value of x =10

In [25]: x
Out[25]: 10
```

Here, the function *int*() converts string '10' to integer 10. We can employ *float*() function to read a real number. The function *float*() convert a string to a real number. For example,

```
In [26]: float(input("Enter the value of x ="))
Enter the value of x =9.7

Out[26]: 9.7
```

The function *str*() does the converse; it converts an integer or a float to a string. For example,

```
In [21]: str(345), str(20.9), str(14.9e10)
Out[21]: ('345', '20.9', '149000000000.0')
```

The function *print*() can print a string, an integer, a float, or a combination of these. For example,

```
In [154]: x=5; y=10.0; z='hello'

In [156]: print('x = ', x,'; ', 'y = ', y, '; ', 'z = ',
z)
x =  5 ;  y =  10.0 ;  z =  hello
```

With this we end our discussion on characters and strings.

****

Exercises

1. What are the outputs of the following Python expressions?
   - 'Jai' + 'Hind', 2*'Hi', 'Hi' + 2020, 2*3*'Hi', 'Hi' + ' friend', 'x'+`y'+'=5'
2. Type भारत, अमेरिका, नमस्ते in your computer. Also type α, β, γ, δ in your computer.
3. What is the output of the following Python statement?
   In [75]: x=5; y=10; print('x+y'); print(x+y)
4. What are the differences between the following two Python statements?
   x = input("Enter the value of x =")
   x = int(input("Enter the value of x ="))

6.2 *List*

We often deal with collections of objects. For example, a classroom has objects such as benches, chairs, blackboards, etc. A school consists of teachers, students, staff, infrastructure, etc. Python offers implementation of such collections using a structure called *list*.

A *list* is a collection of objects. Note that the elements of a list could be of different data types (integer, real, character, string).

```
In [1]: y = [10,20,'hi']
```

In the above example, the list y has 3 elements: 10, 20 (integers), and 'hi' (string). See below for an illustration.

10	20	'hi'

Note that the elements of a list are arranged in a sequence. For example, in the list y, the elements, 10, 20, and 'hi', are respectively the first, second, and third elements of the list, and they can be accessed using y[0], y[1], and y[2] respectively. Here, the integers—0, 1, and 2—are called *indices* of the list y. An important point is that the index starts from 0, not 1.

```
In [2]: print (y[0], y[1], y[2])
10 20 hi
```

Interestingly, the last element of Python can be accessed using y[–1]. In addition, 20 and 10 can be accessed using indices –2 and –3 respectively. Table 6 illustrates the two methods of indexing.

```
In [3]: print (y[-3], y[-2], y[-1])
10 20 hi
```

Table 6: indices of array y

index	0	1	2
index	–3	–2	-1
y	10	20	'hi'

An important question: Why do we need a list when we already have integers, float, and strings in Python?

Answer: A list provides a structure for organising data. For example, we can organise the students of a school in one list, and the teachers in another list. These two lists have different properties. For example, teachers receive their salaries, while students pay fees. Data is much better organised with lists.

Note that the friends' list on social media platforms is similar to a *list*. Such structures make communication so much easier. Interestingly, a string is also a list. For example,

```
In [189]: z = 'Python'

In [191]: z[0], z[1], z[2], z[3], z[4], z[5], z[-1], z[-2]
Out[191]: ('P', 'y', 't', 'h', 'o', 'n', 'n', 'o')
```

The functions associated with a list are displayed in Table 7.

Table 7: List of functions associated with Python *list*.

Function	Description
append(element)	Appends *element* at the end of the list.
pop()	Removes the last *element* from the list and returns this element
pop(i)	Removes the ith element of the list, and returns it.
remove(*element*)	Removes the first occurrence of *element* from the list.
reverse()	Reverses the list.
sort()	Sorts the list.
copy()	Returns a copy of the list.
index(x)	Returns the lowest index of the list where the element x is stored.
count(x)	Returns the number of occurrences of the *element* x in the list.
insert(*ind*,x)	Inserts the element x into the list at index *ind*.

Some examples illustrating the above functions are as follows:

```
In [192]: a = [1, 3, 5, 9, 15]

In [193]: a.append(21)

In [194]: a
Out[194]: [1, 3, 5, 9, 15, 21]

In [196]: a.insert(2,4)

In [197]: a
Out[197]: [1, 3, 4, 5, 9, 15, 21]

In [199]: a.reverse()

In [200]: a
Out[200]: [21, 15, 9, 5, 4, 3, 1]
```

We can change any element of the list. For example, we can change the first element of *a* from 21 to 100 using the following statement.

```
In [212]: a[0]=100

In [213]: a
Out[213]: [100, 15, 9, 5, 4, 3, 1]
```

We can add two lists using + operator.

```
In [203]: a+[0,1]
Out[203]: [21, 15, 9, 5, 4, 3, 1, 0, 1]
```

Two useful list functions of Python are *size*(*a*) and *len*(*a*). Apart from some technical differences, these functions yield the size of a list.

```
In [89]: a = [100, 15, 9, 5, 4, 3, 1]

In [90]: len(a)
Out[90]: 7

In [91]: size(a)
Out[91]: 7
```

Note that a string appears to be like a *list*, but its contents cannot be changed, as shown in the following example. However, you may convert a string to a list using the list function, and then change the contents of the list.

```
In [9]: x='abcd'

In [10]: print(x[0], x[1], x[2], x[-1])
a b c d

In [11]: x[0]='S'

TypeError: 'str' object does not support item assignment

In [12]: x=list('abcd')

In [13]: x
Out[13]: ['a', 'b', 'c', 'd']

In [14]: x[0]='S'

In [15]: x
Out[15]: ['S', 'b', 'c', 'd']
```

The subtle difference between a string and a list is due to the nature of objects, called *mutable* and *immutable*. But this topic is beyond the scope of this book. You can refer to advanced Python books to study this topic.

Slicing

A *sublist* of a list can be accessed by *slicing*. For a list *a*, *a*[*start_i*: *end_i*] yields a sublist [*a*[*start_i*], *a*[*start_i*+1], ... *a*[*end_i*−1]], where *start_i* and *end_i* are integers. Note that the sublist includes *a*[*start_i*] but excludes *a*[*end_i*], and that the number of elements in the sublist is *end_i* −*start_i*.

Example: For *a* = [100, 15, 9, 5, 4, 3, 1],

```
In [306]: a[1:5]
Out[306]: [15, 9, 5, 4]
```

The above sublist has elements *a*[1], *a*[2], *a*[3], *a*[4], but not *a*[5]. Some other slicing rules are as follows:

1. We can pick elements of *a* with gaps. For example, *a*[*i*, *j*, *k*]

yields a sublist from $a[i]$ to $a[j-1]$ in steps of k. If k is omitted, it is set to its default value of 1.

2. $a[:j]$ contains elements $a[0]$, … , $a[j-1]$; while $a[j:]$ contains elements $a[j]$, …, $a[-1]$ (the last element). Thus $a[:i]$ + $a[i:]$ covers the complete array a.
3. The index of –1 is same as the last index, which is $len(x)$–1. Hence, it is logical that $x[:-1]$ yields $x[0,len(x)-1,1]$, which is [100, 15, 9, 5, 4, 3].
4. Python uses special values for the missing arguments of the slice function. For *start, end,* and *step,* use 0, $len(x)$, and 1 respectively. As a result, $x[::]$ yields the full array.

Examples:

```
In [227]: x = [100, 15, 9, 5, 4, 3, 1]

In [228]: x[1:4]
Out[228]: [15, 9, 5]

In [229]: x[1:-1]  # x[-1] is skipped.
Out[229]: [15, 9, 5, 4, 3]

In [230]: x[::]    # from 0 to end
Out[230]: [100, 15, 9, 5, 4, 3, 1]

In [231]: x[::-1]  # step = -1, reverse the array
Out[231]: [1, 3, 4, 5, 9, 15, 100]

In [232]: x[:3] # start = 0, end = 3, step = 1
Out[232]: [100, 15, 9]

In [233]: x[4:]    # start = 4, goes to the end, step = 1
Out[233]: [4, 3, 1]

In [234]: x[4:-1]  #start = 4, end = -1, step = 1
Out[234]: [4, 3]

In [235]: x[4::-1] # start = 4, step = -1, goes up to
start
Out[235]: [4, 5, 9, 15, 100]
```

Function range()

Using *range(start, end, step)* function of Python, we can generate a sequence of integers from *start* to *end*−1 in steps of *step*. In *range()*, *start* and *steps* are optional with their default values as 0 and 1 respectively. For example,

1. *range*(1,10,2) will generate a sequence [1, 3, 5, 7, 9].
2. *range*(5) will generate a sequence [0,1,2,3,4]
3. *range*(1,5) will generate a sequence [1,2,3,4]
4. *range*(5,1,–2) will generate a sequence [5,3]

Tuples

We introduce another Python data structure called *tuple*. *Tuples* are very similar to *lists*, except that the elements of *tuples* cannot be changed. Also, the elements of a tuple are enclosed within small brackets, not square brackets as in lists. For example,

```
In [81]: c=(1,22,3)

In [82]: c[1]
Out[82]: 22
```

We get an error if we attempt to change the elements of *c*, for example, $c[1] = 100$ produces an error. This is because the elements of a tuple cannot be changed. Technically, such objects are called *immutable*, but we will not discuss this issue in this book.

Dictionary

We access an element of a list using its index. However, often we need the reverse feature. In a class, we may need to find the roll number of a student given his/her name. In system programming, we need the memory address given variable name. Python's *dictionary* provides such features with each item as *key-value* pair. For the class, a student's name and roll number form a pair, while the variable's name and address could form a pair for Python's symbol table. The pairs of *key* and its value are stored as *key:value,* and the pairs are separated by commas.

We illustrate the above dictionaries using concrete examples. Consider a dictionary, named *myclass,* that contains three students along with their roll numbers, which are 101, 102, and 103. The roll number (*value*) of a student *x* (*key*) can be accessed using *myclass*[*x*].

```
In [1]: myclass = {'Rahul': 101, 'Arjun':102, 'Krishna':
103}

In [3]: myclass['Rahul']
Out[3]: 101
```

Consider another dictionary *vars* containing Python variables *x and y,* as well as their addresses.

```
In [8]: var = {'x': 4533028272, 'y' : 4533028304}

In [9]: var['x']
Out[9]: 4533028272
```

The dictionaries have the following properties:

1. The keys of a dictionary are unique, but the values may not be.
2. Dictionaries are unordered, and hence the items of a dictionary cannot be accessed using indices. Instead, the value of an item is accessed using its key.
3. Dictionaries are changeable. That is, we can delete an entry of the dictionary; modify an element corresponding to a key; etc. Note that the keys cannot be changed, but they can be deleted.

We illustrate the addition and deletion of items in a dictionary as follows. In the dictionary *myclass,* we add a student named Radha whose roll number is 104. In addition, we delete *Rahul* from the dictionary.

```
In [12]: myclass['Radha'] = 104

In [13]: myclass
Out[13]: {'Rahul': 101, 'Arjun': 102, 'Krishna': 103,
```

```
'Radha': 104}

In [15]: del myclass['Rahul']

In [16]: myclass
Out[16]: {'Arjun': 102, 'Krishna': 103, 'Radha': 104}
```

We can implement a French-to-English dictionary in Python with pairs of French word and its English synonym. For example,

```
In [20]: french_eng = {'bon':'good', 'merci':'thanks you'}

In [21]: french_eng['bon']
Out[21]: 'good'

In [22]: french_eng['Oui'] = 'yes'  # add an entry

In [23]: french_eng
Out[23]: {'bon': 'very good', 'merci': 'thanks you',
'Oui': 'yes'}
```

We can also create a dictionary using Python loop:

```
In [9]: sqr = {x: x**2 for x in (2, 4, 6, 8)}

In [10]: sqr
Out[10]: {2: 4, 4: 16, 6: 36, 8: 64}
```

With this we end our discussion on Python's list, tuple, and dictionary.

****

Conceptual questions

1. List the properties of a Python *list*.
2. Why do we need a *list* in Python when we already have integers, floats, and strings in Python?
3. Zero (0) is a valid address for computer memory. Why don't we adopt this convention for house numbering?
4. What are the differences between Python's *list*, *tuple*, and

dictionary?

Exercises

1. Given a Python list y = [0, 1, 2, 3, 4, 5, 6], what are the outputs for the following operations?
    - *y*[0], *y*[2], *y*[10], *y*[0:2], *y*[1:3], *y*[2:–1], *y*[:–1], *y*[::–1], *y*[:2], *y*[-1:3],*y*[-1:3:-1]
2. What are the outputs of the following Python statements?
    - range(10), range(1,10), range(1,10,3), range(5,1,–1)
3. Given a list y = [0, 2, 4, 6], what are the Python outputs for the following list operations? For each operation, start with the original y.
    - y.pop(), y.append(10), y.reverse(), y.insert(2,3)
4. Consider a string s = "The Earth". What are the outputs of s[0], s[2], s[3], s[–1], s[-2]?
5. Construct a Python dictionary whose keys are (1,2,3,4,5) and the corresponding values are the cubes of the keys.
6. Construct a Python dictionary that mimics the English-Hindi language dictionary. Take any 5 words. Type Hindi words in Devnagari script.

6.3 Numpy Arrays

Numpy arrays of Python are similar to lists, but with some major differences. The elements of a numpy array are of the same data type. That is, they are all integers or all float. In addition, the array elements are stored in consecutive memory locations. These features of numpy arrays make them faster than list. We will list more differences in later parts of this section.

The function *array*() creates a numpy array of integers or real numbers (float). We remark that such arrays and the associated array operations are functions of *Numpy* (numerical python) module of Python, that is why these arrays are called *Numpy arrays*. In the following examples, we describe how to declare an *array* and how to access its elements. Note that just like a *list*, the elements of an *array* have their assigned locations in the array. Hence, *array* elements are accessed by their indices.

```
In [265]: y=array([5,9]) # Creates an array with elements
5 and 9

In [266]: y[1]
Out[266]: 9

In [268]: y*2    # Multiply each array element by 2
Out[268]: array([10, 18])

In [269]: size(y)  # yields count of elements in the array
Out[269]: 2

In [270]: len(y)   # provides length of the array
Out[270]: 2

In [271]: z = y+3   # Add 3 to each array element

In [272]: z
Out[272]: array([ 8, 12])
```

In a hybrid array containing integers and float, Numpy converts all the elements to float. Note that unlike a *list*, we cannot insert an element in an array or delete an element from an array. For example, y.append(10) is an invalid operation for an array *y*.

We can perform *real* operations on the array elements using functions *sqrt, log, log10, sin, cos,* etc. Note that these functions operate on each element of the array. For example,

```
In [265]: y=array([5,9])

In [448]: sqrt(y)
Out[448]: array([2.23606798, 3.])
```

The +, *, / operations on two arrays yield respective element-by-element addition, multiplication, and division.

```
In [449]: z = array([1.0,4.0])

In [450]: y+z
Out[450]: array([ 6., 13.])

In [451]: y*z
Out[451]: array([ 5., 36.])

In [452]: y/z
Out[452]: array([5.   , 2.25])
```

The functions *sum*(*a*) for an array provides the sum of all the elements of the array, while *prod*(*a*) provides the product of all its elements. These functions work for integer as well as float arrays.

```
In [7]: a=array([2,3,6])

In [8]: sum(a)
Out[8]: 11

In [9]: prod(a)
Out[9]: 36
```

Also note that a list can be converted to a numpy array as follows:

```
In [312]: y=[3,4]

In [313]: array(y)
Out[313]: array([3, 4])
```

Similarly, we can convert a numpy array to a *list* using the *list*() function:

```
In [21]: z=array([10,20])

In [22]: list(z)
Out[22]: [10, 20]
```

Functions *linspace*() and *arange*()

The numpy functions *linspace*() *and arange*() create useful arrays. They are described below:

linspace(*start, stop, n*): It returns *n* uniformly distributed real numbers from *start* to *stop*. All the three arguments are mandatory for linspace().

arange(*start, stop, step*): It returns numbers from *start* to *stop* (excluding) in steps of *step*. The arguments *start* and *step* are optional with their default values as 0 and 1 respectively. The function *arange*() is float equivalent to the function *range*() that returns an integer list. Note that the *range*() function cannot take a real number as an argument. For example, *range*(10.0) gives an error.

We illustrate the above functions using the following examples.

```
In [11]: linspace(1,10,6)
Out[11]: array([ 1. ,  2.8,  4.6,  6.4,  8.2, 10. ])

In [12]: arange(1,10,1.5)  # excludes 10
Out[12]: array([1. , 2.5, 4. , 5.5, 7. , 8.5])

In [13]: arange(10)
Out[13]: array([0, 1, 2, 3, 4, 5, 6, 7, 8, 9])

In [14]: arange(4,10)
Out[14]: array([4, 5, 6, 7, 8, 9])
```

Example 1: The average monthly temperatures of a city for twelve months starting from January are 5, 9, 15, 20, 35, 40, 39, 34, 27, 22, 10, 9 Celcius. To represent this data we employ two arrays.

```
In [8]: month = linspace(1,12,12)

In [9]: month
```

```
Out[9]: array([ 1.,  2.,  3.,  4.,  5.,  6.,  7.,  8.,
9., 10., 11., 12.])

In [15]: temperature = array([5, 9, 15, 20, 35, 40, 39,
34, 27, 22, 10, 9])

In [16]: temperature
Out[16]: array([ 5,  9, 15, 20, 35, 40, 39, 34, 27, 22,
10,  9])
```

In Section 11.2 we show how to make the temperature vs. month plot. Note that we can also implement the above data using Python dictionary as well.

```
In [18]: tempr = {1:5, 2:9, 3:15, 4:20, 5:35, 6:40, 7:39,
8:34, 9:27, 10:22, 11:10, 12:9}

In [19]: tempr[2]   # temperature of the second month
Out[20]: 9
```

Multi-dimensional arrays

The following examples illustrate how to create two-dimensional arrays and associated numpy functions. We create a two-dimensional array *x* as follows:

```
In [25]: x=array([[4,5,6], [7,8,9]])

In [26]: x
Out[26]:
array([[4, 5, 6],
       [7, 8, 9]])
```

The array *x* has 6 elements arranged in 2 rows and 3 columns as shown below.

4	5	6
7	8	9

We can access the elements of a 2D array using [*i,j*] or [*i*][*j*], where *i* and *j* are two indices. The first index represents the row, while the second index represents the column. A diagram representing the variations of the two indices of array x is shown below. Both the indices start from 0.

[0,0]	[0,1]	[0,2]
[1,0]	[1,1]	[1,2]

In memory, the data is stored in sequence as [0,0], [0,1], [0,2], [1,0], [1,1], and [1,2]. Here, the column index moves faster than the row index. Note that the array elements also can be accessed as [0][0], [0][1], [0][2], [1][0], [1][1], and [1][2]. That is, $x[0,1]$ and $x[0][1]$ yield the same element.

```
In [320]: print(x[0,1], x[0][1])
5, 5
```

Three-dimensional arrays are created in a similar manner. For example,

```
In [100]: y = array([[[1, 2], [3, 4]], [[5, 6], [7, 8]]])

In [101]: y
Out[101]:
array([[[1, 2],
        [3, 4]],

       [[5, 6],
        [7, 8]]])

In [102]: y[1,1,1]
Out[102]: 8
```

In this book, we will not discuss three-dimensional arrays in more detail.

Creation of an array

The following Numpy functions are used to extract the size and shape of an array, and to create new arrays of specific kind.

size(a): Returns the number of elements of array *a*.

size(a, *axis_ind*): Returns the number of elements of array *a* along axis *axis_ind* that starts from 0.

shape(a): Returns the shape of array *a*. The *shape* is a tuple with number of elements along each axis.

zeros(*shape*): Returns a new array of zeros of a given *shape*.

ones(*shape*): Returns a new array of ones of a given *shape*.

empty(*shape*): Returns a new array of given *shape* without initializing the entries.

Example 2:

```
In [357]: a = ones((3,3))

In [358]: a
Out[358]:
array([[1., 1., 1.],
       [1., 1., 1.],
       [1., 1., 1.]])

In [359]: size(a)
Out[359]: 9

In [360]: shape(a)
Out[360]: (3, 3)

In [28]: size(a,1) #size along axis 1
Out[28]: 3

In [57]: zeros((2,3))
Out[57]:
array([[0., 0., 0.],
       [0., 0., 0.]])

In [58]: ones((2,1))
Out[58]:
array([[1.],
       [1.]])
```

Example 3: We could store the month and temperature data of

Example 1 in a single two-dimensional array as follows. Here, the first column represents the month, while the second column the temperature.

```
In [19]: temperature  = zeros((12,2))

In [25]: temperature[:,0] =  linspace(1,12,12)

In [26]: temperature[:,1] =  array([ 5,  9, 15, 20, 35,
40, 39, 34, 27, 22, 10,  9])

In [27]: temperature
Out[27]:
array([[ 1.,   5.],
       [ 2.,   9.],
       [ 3.,  15.],
       [ 4.,  20.],
       [ 5.,  35.],
       [ 6.,  40.],
       [ 7.,  39.],
       [ 8.,  34.],
       [ 9.,  27.],
       [10.,  22.],
       [11.,  10.],
       [12.,   9.]])
```

With this we end our discussion on numpy arrays.

****

Conceptual questions

1. What are the differences between a *list* and a *numpy array*?

Exercises

1. Consider an array $x = array([2,4,6,8,10])$. What are the outputs of $x[1]$, $x[3]$, $x[-1]$?

2. For the array $x = array([1,2,3,4,5])$, what are the outputs of $sqrt(x)$ and x**2?
3. What is the outputs of *linspace*(0,10,11) and *arange*(0,10,1)?
4. Write a Python code to construct a 3x3 two-dimensional array whose elements are $A[i,j] = (i+1)*(j+1)$.

Chapter Seven
PROGRAM STRUCTURES

Synopsis

"Most good programmers do programming not because they expect to get paid or get adulation by the public, but because it is fun to program"
— Linus Torvalds

This chapter describes basic program structures: statements, conditionals, and loops.

7.1 Simple Statements

The smallest unit of any computer program is one of the following types:

1. Simple sequential statements
2. Conditional or branching statements
3. Repetitive structure

In the present and next two sections, we will cover these structures along with some simple examples. The present section describes sequential statements.

A Python code segment may contain statements written one after the other. This kind of code segment belongs to category 1 (Simple sequential statements). These statements are executed in the same sequence as in the code. For example, the following code segment consists of three Python statements, which are separated by semicolons (;).

```
In [482]: x=5; \
     ...: y=10; \
     ...: print(x,' ' ,y)
5  10
```

Another example of sequential statements is given below. This code segment swaps two numbers a and b.

```
In [207]: a, b = 5,6

In [208]: tmp = a; a = b; b = tmp

In [209]: a,b
Out[209]: (6, 5)
```

A simple and more straightforward method to swap two numbers is as follows:

```
In [212]: a, b = 5,6

In [213]: b, a = a,b
```

```
In [214]: a,b
Out[214]: (6, 5)
```

Sequential statements are quite simple. We end this discussion here.

****

Exercises

1. Write a program to solve an equation $a\,x^2 + b\,x + c = 0$. Read the values of the parameters *a,b,c* (assume real) from the keyboard.
2. A projectile is fired straight up with a velocity v. Write a Python code that prints the height achieved by this projectile, as well as the time taken to reach there.
3. A projectile is fired with velocity v at an angle θ. Write a Python code to compute the trajectory (that is y as a function of x) of the projectile.

7.2 Conditional Flow in Python

In a computer program, as well as in life, we perform operations based on certain conditions. For example, if hungry, we eat food, else skip our meal. In this section, we describe various types of conditional flows in Python.

if statement

The following Python segment illustrates use of an *if statement*. See Figure 27 for an illustration of the corresponding conditional flow.

```
In [491]: x = 3

In [492]: if (x%2 == 1):
     ...:     print('x is odd')
     ...:
x is odd
```

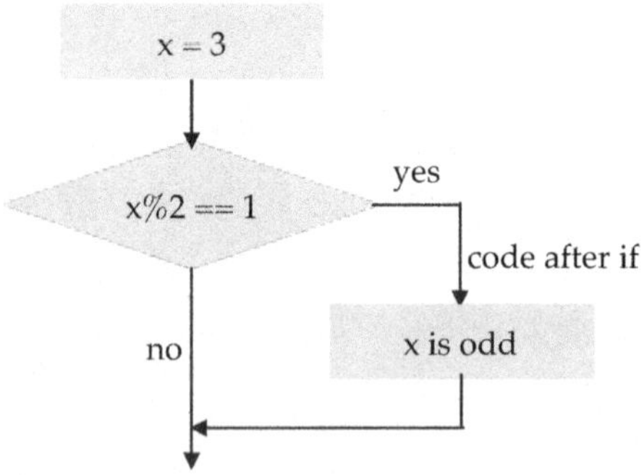

Figure 27: Conditional flow for an *if statement*. The rhombus contains the condition for the *if statement*.

In the above code segment, *if (x%2 == 1)* is a conditional statement. The subsequent statement, *print('x is odd')*, is executed only if the logical expression ($x\%2 == 1$) is *True*. For example, the print statement will be executed for $x = 3$, but not for $x = 4$. You can test it yourself. The diagram in Figure 27 illustrates the control flow the code segment.

Hence, such a diagram is called a *control-flow diagram*. In the diagram, the rhombus contains the conditional statement, while the square boxes contain simple statements.

The indentation (blank spaces) of the *"print('x is odd')"* statement tells the Python interpreter what to execute after the *if statement*. We can put as many statements as required below the *if statement* with indentation. All these statements will be executed when the condition of the *if statement* is *True*. An improper indentation will, of course, give an error.

if-else statement

Now we illustrate the conditional flow for *if-else statements*. See Figure 28 for an illustration.

```
In [493]: x = 2

In [500]: if (x%2 == 1):
     ...:     print('x is odd')
     ...: else:
     ...:     print('x is even')
     ...:
x is even
```

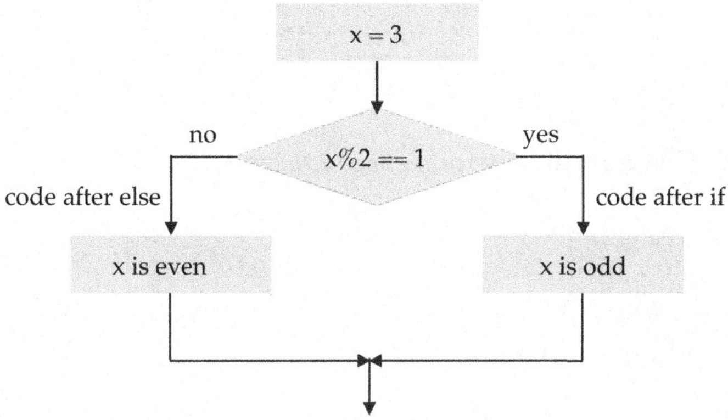

Figure 28: Conditional flow for *if-else statements*.

In the above code segment, the first print statement ('*x is odd*') is executed if ($x\%2 == 1$) is *True*. Otherwise, the second print statement ('*x is even*'), which is after *else statement,* is executed.

if-elif-else statement

Note that the program segments in the *if* and *else* branches may themselves contain further conditional statements. In the example below, among the odd numbers, we further test if the number *x* is divisible by 3 or not (see Figure 29).

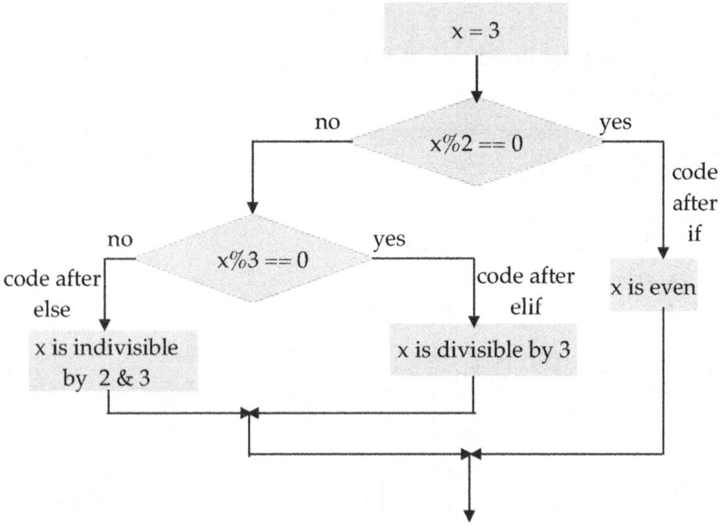

Figure 29: Conditional flow for *if-elif-else statements.*

```
In [501]: x = 27

In [502]: if (x%2 == 0):
    ...:     print('x is even')
    ...: elif(x%3 == 0):
    ...:     print('x is divisible by 3')
    ...: else:
    ...:     print('x is indivisible by 2 & 3')
```

```
...:
```

x is divisible by 3

Example 1: Given the three sides of a triangle, *a, b, c,* we write a Python code to classify the triangle as equilateral or isosceles or neither of the two. The program is as follows:

```
In [2]: a = 6; b=8; c=7

In [3]: if (a == b):
   ...:     if (b==c):
   ...:         print("equilateral triangle")
   ...:     else:
   ...:         print("isosceles triangle") # (a = b) != c
   ...: elif (b == c):  #note a != b
   ...:     print("isosceles triangle") # (b = c) != a
   ...: else:
   ...:     print("neither equilateral nor isosceles")
   ...:
neither equilateral nor isosceles
```

The logic of the program is quite obvious. One can easily check the correctness of the code.

Example 2: We write a Python program that identifies a leap year. We employ the following logic for the same. Consider year = yr.

```
If yr is divisible by 400
   then yr is  a leap year
else if yr is divisible by 100
   then yr is not a leap year
else if yr is divisible by 4
   then yr is  a leap year
else yr is  not a leap year
```

Python code for the above computation is as follows.

```
In [37]: yr = 1984

In [61]: if (yr%400 == 0):
    ...:     print ('A leap year')
    ...: elif(yr%100 == 0):
    ...:     print ('Not a leap year')
    ...: elif(yr%4 == 0):
```

```
   ...:     print ('A leap year')
   ...: else:
   ...:     print ('Not a leap year')
```

A shorter and cryptic code is as follows:

```
In [37]: yr = 1984
In [39]: if (yr%400 == 0):
    ...:     print('A leap year')
    ...: elif (yr%4 ==0) and ~(yr%100==0):
    ...:     print('A leap year')
    ...: else:
    ...:     print('Not a leap year')
    ...:
A leap year
```

With this, we end our discussion on conditional structures in Python.

****

Exercises

1. *Perfect square* is a number whose square root is an integer. Examples of perfect squares are 25, 36. Write a Python code to test if a number is perfect square or not.
2. *Armstrong number* is a number that is equal to the sum of cube of its digits. One such number is 153, which is $1^3+3^3+5^3$. Write a Python program that tests if a number is an Armstrong number or not. Hint: Use the functions *str*() and *int*() discussed in Chapter Six.
3. A *palindrome string* is one that reads the same forward and backward. Examples of palindrome strings are 'lal', 'KAK', '010'. Write a Python code that tests whether a string is a palindrome or not.
4. Write a Python program to test if a triangle is a right-angle triangle.

7.3 *Looping in Python*

Many processes repeat themselves. For example, Earth goes around the Sun. Seasons repeat after a year. A student goes to school every working day. In python, repetitive tasks can be implemented using *for loops* and *while loops*. We will describe them below.

for loops

The structure of a *for loop* is as follows:

```
for an element in list:
   body of the loop
```

The body of the loop is executed for all the elements of the list. We illustrate the loop structures using the following examples.

Example 1: The following Python code prints the names of all the students in the *student_list*.

```
In [508]: student_list = ['Rahul', 'Mohan', 'Shyam',
'Shanti']

In [509]: for student in student_list:
     ...:     print(student, '\n')
     ...:
Rahul

Mohan

Shyam

Shanti
```

Figure 30 illustrates the working of the *for* loop. The loop is carried out for all students in the list. The loop starts with the first student and continues till the *student_list* is exhausted. Note that the initialisation (index = 0) and index increment (index = index+1) take place inside the loop automatically.

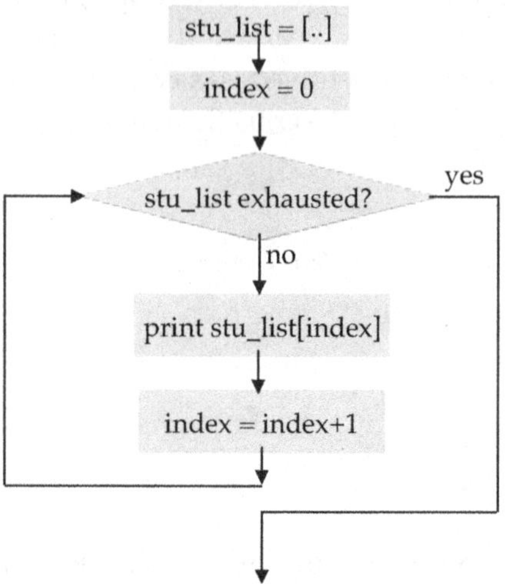

Figure 30: Illustration of the *for* loop of Example 1.

Example 2: Compute *factorial*(n) using for loop.

```
In [510]: n = 5
     ...: fact=1
     ...: for i in range(2,n+1):
     ...:     fact = fact*i
     ...:

In [511]: print("Factorial of ", n, '= ', fact)
Factorial of  5 =  120
```

In this example, *range*(2,n+1) creates a list containing integers 2 to n (excluding n+1). Hence, the *for loop* is carried out for i from 2 to n.

Example 3: Find the maximum number in a list.

```
In [42]: A =  [6, 0, 4, 9, 3]

In [43]: max = A[0]
```

```
In [44]: for i in range(2, len(A)):
    ...:     if (A[i] > max):
    ...:         max = A[i]
    ...:

In [45]: max
Out[45]: 9
```

In this example, the loop is carried out for *i* from 2 to the end of the list *A*. Here, we follow the algorithm of Example 2 of Chapter Two. We set *max* = *A*[0]. After this, we compare *max* with *A*[1]. If *A*[1] > *max*, *max* = *A*[1], else *max* remains as *A*[0]. We continue this comparison for the next array element, and so on. At the end of the loop, *max* is the largest number of the array.

Example 4: In an integer array, send the maximum element to the end of the array.

```
n [46]: A =  [6, 0, 4, 9, 3]

In [47]: for i in range(len(A)-1):
    ...:      if (A[i] > A[i+1]):
    ...:          A[i], A[i+1] = A[i+1], A[i]
    ...:

In [48]: A
Out[48]: [0, 4, 6, 3, 9]
```

In this example, we follow similar logic as Example 3. Among *A*[*i*] and *A*[*i*+1], the larger number is pushed to the right. The loop is carried out from *i* = 0 to *n*–2, where *n* is the length of the array *A*. The above process is similar to the bubbling operation in which the lightest element rises to the top. This idea is used in bubble sort (see Section 9.2).

while loops

The structure of a *while loop* is as follows:

```
while expression:
  Body of the while loop
```

The body of the *while* loop is executed until the *expression* remains *True*. The loop is terminated as soon as the condition becomes *False*. We illustrate the structure of the while loop using several examples.

Example 5: Computes *factorial*(n) using while loop.

```
In [514]: n = 5
     ...: fact = 1
     ...: i = 2
     ...: while (i <= n):
     ...:     fact = fact*i
     ...:     i = i+1
     ...:
```

The *while* loop is executed until the running index $i<=n$. The loop terminates as soon as i exceeds n. See Figure 31 for an illustration.

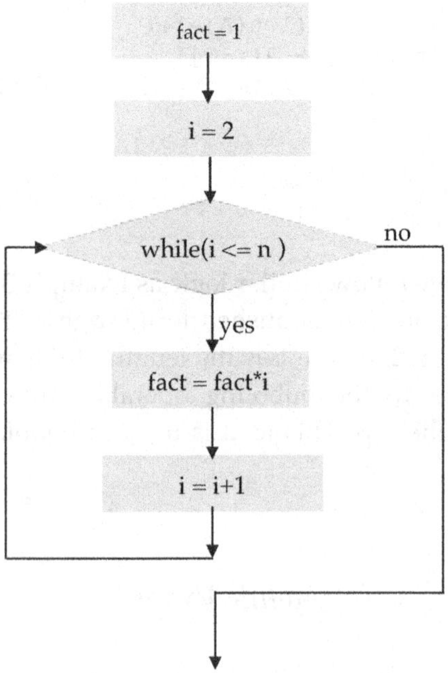

Figure 31: Illustration of the *while* loop of Example 5.

Example 6: Compute the greatest common divisor (gcd) of two integers a and b using Euclid's algorithm.

```
In [525]: a, b = 2277, 1633

In [526]: while b:
     ...:     a, b = b, a%b
     ...:
In [527]: print(a)
23
```

In the above algorithm we assume that $b < a$. During the iteration, $a \leftarrow b$ and $b \leftarrow a\%b$. This loop is continued until $b = 0$. Refer to wikipedia for more details on Euclid's algorithm.

Infinite loop and *break* statement

A programmer needs to make sure that all the loops of a program terminate. Otherwise, the non-terminating loop and, hence, the program will continue forever. Such a loop is called an *infinite loop*. An example of an infinite loop is given below.

```
In [54]: i=1

In [55]: while (i>0):
    ...:     i = i+1
    ...:
```

It is straightforward to verify that the above loop does not terminate. We will have to kill the program by pressing Cntrl-C (control-C). Every programmer must ensure that their code does not have an infinite loop.

At the end, we introduce a *break* statement, which is a useful Python construct to exit a loop. We illustrate an application of the break statement using the following example.

Example 7: A program that reads positive integers in a loop. The loop terminates when a negative number is encountered.

```
In [186]: while(True):
     ...:     x = input()
     ...:     if (int(x) < 0):
     ...:         break
     ...:
4
5
100
-1
```

In this example, the loop terminates when $x = -1$. On a practical note, a *breaking* component can be used to stop an instrument when it faces a catastrophe. A fuse in a circuit board is an example of such a component. When the electric current exceeds a certain limit (for example, 15 Amperes), the fuse melts and cuts off the power supply, thus saving our homes/appliances from damage.

for... else

An *else* structure after a *for loop* or a *while loop* is an interesting feature of Python. The *else* block is executed when the loop finishes normally. We illustrate this structure using an example. In the following code we test if a number n is a prime or not. Here, we use a property that one of the factors of a non-prime number must be less than equal to $\sqrt{n}$.

```
n=15

# i ranges from 2 to sqrt(n) in steps of 1.
for i in range(2, int(sqrt(n))+1):
  if (n%i == 0):
    print ("n is divisible by ", i)
    print("Hence, n not  a prime")
    break
else:
  print ("n is a prime")
```

In the above code, the *else* block is coupled to the *if* statement inside the loop. The *for-else* structure provides a clean way to contrast nonprime numbers with prime numbers. Try to write the above code without the else structure.

In the next chapter we will discuss *functions* in Python.

****

Conceptual questions

1. What are the differences between a *for loop* and a *while loop*?

Exercises

1. Write a Python code to find the minimum number in a list of numbers.
2. Write your own Python function to sum the elements of a numpy array using a loop structure.
3. Write a Python code to sum the digits of an integer. Example: for 456, the answer is 4+5+6 = 15.
4. Write your own Python code to convert a binary number to a decimal number. Assume the number to be a positive integer with no sign bit.
5. Write a Python code to construct a 5x5 two-dimensional array $A[i,j] = (i+1)*(j+1)$.
6. Pingala-Virahanka-Fibonacci numbers are defined as follows: $f(n) = f(n-1) + f(n-2)$ with starting sequence as $f(0) = 1$ and $f(1) = 1$. Write a Python program to compute the first 15 Pingala-Virahanka-Fibonacci numbers.
7. Iterate the function $x_{n+1} = f(x_n)$ where $f(x) = 4x(1-x)$. Generate the sequences for $x_0 = 0.3$. How does the behaviour change when $f(x) = ax(1-x)$ with $a = 0.5, 1.5, 3.1, 3.5$.

Chapter Eight
FUNCTIONS IN PYTHON

Synopsis

"Doing mathematics should always mean finding patterns and crafting beautiful and meaningful explanations." — Albert Einstein

In this chapter, we describe how to write Python functions.

8.1 Functions in Python

We encounter functions in mathematics. A function takes inputs and produces outputs. For example, a function $f(x) = x^2$ takes a number as an input and provides its square as an output. Note that a function can take several inputs and produce several outputs. An example of a function with several inputs and outputs is $f(x,y) = (x^2 + y^2,\ x^3 + y^3)$; it takes two inputs (x,y) and generates two outputs $(x^2 + y^2,\ x^3 + y^3)$. See Figure 32 for an illustration of a mathematical function.

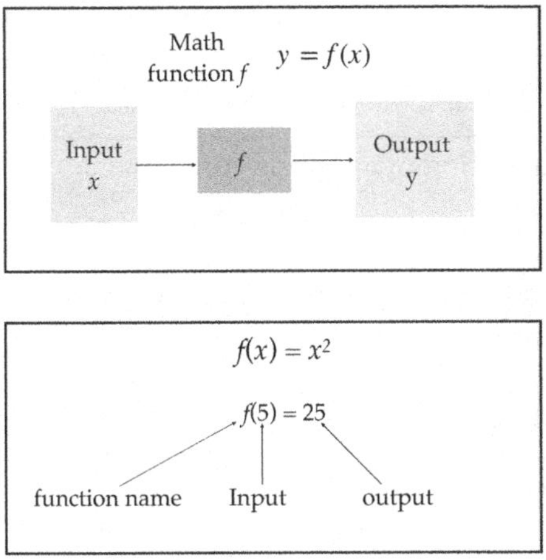

Figure 32: An illustration of a mathematical function.

We similarly define a Python function. A Python function takes inputs, called *parameters*, and returns outputs after computation. A python function typically appears as follows:

```
def function_name (parameters):
    Body of the function
    Typically includes a return statement
```

See Figure 33 for an illustration. A Python function generates output via its *return* statement, which is usually present inside the function. Note that some functions may not have a *return* statement.

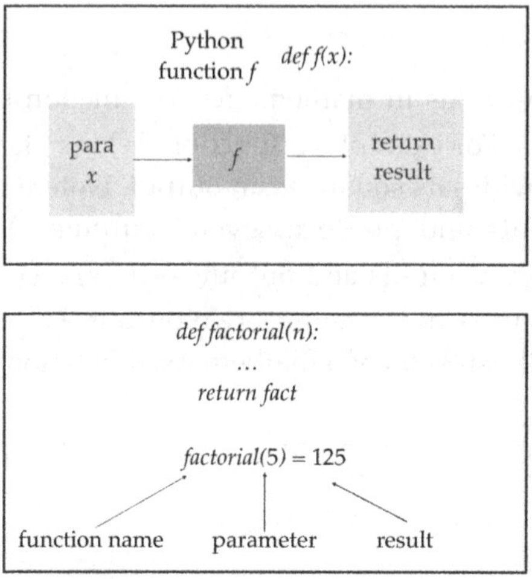

Figure 33: An illustration of a Python function.

Example 1: The following Python function *factorial*(*n*) that returns *n*!. Note the statement *return fact*.

```
def factorial(n):
    fact = 1
    for i in range(2,n+1):
        fact = fact*i
    return fact
```

```
Usage:

In [16]: factorial(8)
Out[16]: 40320

In [17]: factorial(9)
Out[17]: 362880
```

Note that we execute the function by typing the function name and providing it with an argument. In the above example, the statement *factorial*(8) executes the Python function *factorial* with argument 8.

Example 2: A Python function that returns the maximum value of a list or an array, denoted by *A*.

```
# Returns maximum number of an array A.
def max_array(A):
    my_max =  A[0]
    for i in range(1,len(A)):
        if (A[i] > my_max):
            my_max = A[i]

    return my_max
```

Usage:

```
In [40]: a = [5, 0, 9, 4]

In [40]: max_array(a)
Out[93]: 9

In [40]: N = array([1.1, 0.9, 0.05])    # numpy array

In [41]: max_array(N)
Out[41]: 1.1

In [45]: B =  ['ab', 'd']

In [46]: max_array(B)
Out[46]: 'd'

In [47]: max(B)       # max is Python function
Out[47]: 'd'
```

Note that we can employ the function *max_array(a)* to a list of strings as well. For two strings, the comparison is performed character by character. That is, 'a' < 'b', and 'ab' < 'd'. In the latter, the second character 'b' of 'ab' is ignored. Note that our function *max_array*() has the same functionality as Python function *max*().

Example 3: A function that sum the digits of an integer.

```
# Returns sum of the digits of n
def sum_digits(n):
    digits_n = list(str(n))
    # list of digits of n [Char entries]
    my_sum = 0
    for k in digits_n:
```

```
        my_sum += int(k)

    return my_sum

In [94]: sum_digits(456)
Out[94]: 15
```

Note that the function *str*(*n*) converts integer *n* to a string of digits, while *int*(*k*) converts a digit (e.g., '1') to an integer. These functions demonstrate the versatility of Python.

Example 4: The following function tests whether a string is a palindrome or not. A palindrome string is one that reads the same forward and backward. Examples are 'lal', 'KAK', '010'.

```
# A Palindrome string is one that is same as its inverse.
# is_palindrome(x) returns 1 if x is Palindrome, 0
otherwise

def is_palindrome(x):
    return(x == x[::-1])

In [100]: is_palindrome('ABCD')
Out[100]: False

In [101]: is_palindrome('ABCCBA')
Out[101]: True
```

In the above function, *x*[::−1] generates a reversed string. See Section 6.2 for an explanation.

Python functions provide many benefits. Once a function has been written and tested, it can be used again and again. A user needs to think only about the interface with the function, that is, its arguments and output; She can safely ignore the details within the function. For example, we use Python functions *sqrt*(), *array*(), *log*(), etc. without worrying about the internal details of these functions.

Variables inside the functions differ from those outside the function. We discuss these details below.

Scopes of Python variables

A Python function has its internal variables. For example, the internal variables of the program of Example 1 are *fact* and *i;* and those of Example 3 are *digits_n, my_sum,* and *k*. These internal variables exist inside the function only, hence, they cannot be accessed outside the function. For these reasons, these variables are called *local variables*.

On the contrary, the variables outside the function, which are called *global variables,* are visible inside a function. However, the global variables cannot be modified inside a function, unless it is declared as a *global* variable inside the function (e.g., *global z,* where *z* is a global variable). We illustrate these variables using an example.

```
In [148]: def myfunc(x):
     ...:     y = x**2
     ...:     print('Inside function: ', x, ' ',y)
     ...:     print('Global var z: ', z)
     ...:

In [149]: y =10

In [150]: z = 999

In [151]: myfunc(y)
Inside function:  10   100
Global var z:  999
```

In the above example, *y* and *z* of *In* [149, 150] are global variables, whose values are 10 and 999 respectively. However, the variable *y* within the function *myfunc*(*x*) is local to the function *myfunc*(), and it has nothing to do with the global variable *y*. Note that the global variable *z* is accessible inside the function. Also note that global variable *z* cannot be modified inside *myfunc(x)*. For example, we cannot write *z*=*z*+2 inside the function. To modify *z*, we need to write *global z* inside the function.

Using Python files

Small Python programs and functions can be typed on Python

interpreter itself. However, it is difficult and impractical to type long programs/functions within a Python interpreter. It is best to write such a program in a separate file and then execute it using a *run* command. Note that Python files have *.py* extension. For example, a file name could be *my_factorial.py*. The suffix *my* is to contrast the function *my_factorial* with Python's *factorial* function.

In Section *1.2*, we showed how to create a Python file using an editor. After creation of a file, it could be executed in *ipython* window using *run* command. I strongly urge you to read the subsection "Creating a Python file using an editor" in Section *1.2*.

After a function has been executed in *ipython* window using the *run* command, it is now available to the interpreter for further use. See below how the function *sum_of_digits*() is executed in *ipython* window.

```
In [115]: run sum_of_digits.py

In [116]: sum_digit(128)
  Out[116]: 11
```

A word of caution is in order here. Recall that ipython was invoked with an option - -pylab, which enables imports of *numpy* and *matplotlib* modules. The *matplotlib* module contains plotting functions. Note that these modules are not available to the file *sum_of_digits.py* by default. The function *sum_digits*() does not need any numpy function, hence we are safe. But, often we will need to invoke some math or plotting functions (for example, *sqrt*()) inside the file itself. In that case, we need to add the following lines in the python file at the top and invoke the requisite function as *np.fn*(). See the statements below.

```
import numpy as np

X = np.sqrt(5)
```

We will encounter such statements while discussing prime numbers in Section 9.1.

In the next section we will discuss recursive functions, which have special properties

****

Conceptual questions

1. What are the benefits of Python functions?

Exercises

1. Write a function that returns the number of elements of a list. Do not use Python's functions *len*() or *size*().
2. Write a function that returns the second-lowest number of list. Example: For a list (e.g., [7, 9, 1, 1, 7]), return 7.
3. For a given array, write a function that returns the smallest number along with its frequency. Example: For a list [7, 9, 1, 1, 7], return (1, 2).
4. Write a Python function that returns the maximum number of a two-dimensional array, which is provided as an input.
5. Write a function that takes a positive decimal integer as an input and returns its binary equivalent. Implement the algorithm detailed in 3.2, rather than using *bin*() function
6. Write a function that takes a positive binary number as an input and returns its decimal equivalent.
7. Pingala-Virahanka-Fibonacci sequence is defined as follows: $f(n) = f(n-1) + f(n-2)$ with $f(0) = 1$ and $f(1) = 1$. Write a Python function to compute $f(n)$.
8. A *strong number* is a number that matches with the sum of the factorials of its digits. Example: 145 = 1! + 4! + 5! = 1 + 24+120. Write a computer function that takes a number as a parameter and returns 1 if the given number is a strong number, and 0 otherwise.
9. Write a Python function that takes an integer n as an input, and generates all the strong numbers from 1 to n.
10. A projectile is fired with speed u and angle θ. Write a Python function that takes u and θ as parameters and returns the range and height of the projectile.

8.2 Recursive Functions

In mathematics, a *recursive function* is one that is defined in terms of itself. For example, *n*! or *factorial*(*n*) is defined in terms of factorial itself:

```
n! = n  (n-1)! for n > 1, and

1! = 1
```

Let us illustrate how the above function works for $n = 3$. By definition, 3! = 3 x 2!, 2! = 2 x 1!, and 1! = 1. The last condition terminates the recursive process, without which we would have had 1! = 1x0!, ..., and so on. After the last step, reverse substitution yields 2! = 2 and 3! = 3x2 – 6, which is the answer.

Recursive function definitions are permitted in Python and in many modern languages (e.g., C, C++, Java). We illustrate this Python feature using several examples.

Example 1: A recursive implementation of factorial(*n*) in Python is as follows.

```
def factorial(n):
    if (n==1):
        return 1
    else:
        return n*factorial(n-1)
```

As described in the earlier discussion,

```
factorial(3) = 3*factorial(2),
factorial(2) = 2*factorial(1),
factorial(1) = 1.
```

After this, reverse substitution yields

```
factorial(2) = 2*1 = 2,
factorial(3) = 3*2 = 6.
```

The function returns 6 as an answer. As expected, the above recursive implementation of *factorial*(n) yields the same result as the iterative solution (Example 1 of the previous section). Note however that the recursive version is quite expensive because it makes forward calls to itself, and then performs reverse substitutions.

Let us consider a more complex problem, *Tower of Hanoi*, for which recursion provides a simple solution.

Example 2: *Tower of Hanoi*: Consider 3 pegs, A, B, C, as shown in the initial configuration of Figure 34. Peg A has n discs, but pegs B and C have none. We need to transfer n disks from peg A to peg C while obeying the following rules:

1. Only one disk can be moved at a time.
2. Only the top disk of a peg can be moved.
3. A larger disk can not be placed on top of a smaller disk.

A recursive solution to achieve this objective is as follows. For $n > 1$,

1. Transfer $n-1$ disks from A to B.
2. Transfer one remaining disk from A to C.
3. Transfer $n-1$ disks from B to C.

When $n = 1$, the disc can be transferred in a single step as long as rule 3 is obeyed. See Figure 34 for an illustration of the above three steps. At the end of the above process, we have n disks at peg C. The recursive Python implementation of the tower of hanoi (toh) is as follows.

```
# Transfer n disks from "source" to "to"
# "intermediate" peg is the secondary peg

def toh(n,source,dest,intermediate):
    if (n==1):
        print("transfer disk ", source , " dest ", dest)
    else:
        toh(n-1, source, intermediate, dest)
        print("transfer disk ", source , " dest ", dest)
        toh(n-1, intermediate, dest, source)
```

```
In [2]: run tower_of_hanoi
```

```
In [3]: toh(3,"A","B","C")
transfer disk  A  to  B
transfer disk  A  to  C
transfer disk  B  to  C
transfer disk  A  to  B
transfer disk  C  to  A
transfer disk  C  to  B
transfer disk  A  to  B
```

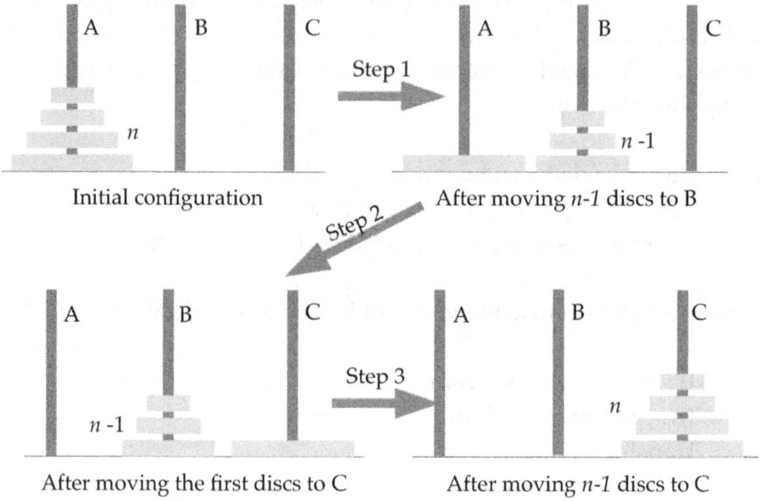

Figure 34: Illustrations of the three steps for solving the tower of Hanoi problem.

In the function definition, we use *source, dest* (for destination), and *intermediate* as the peg labels. This is because source, destination, and intermediate pegs vary at different stages of function calls.

For the above algorithm, we state without proof that the number of moves required to transfer n disks is 2^n-1.

Example 3: Pingala-Virahanka-Fibonacci (PVF) sequence is defined recursively as

$$f(n) = f(n-1) + f(n-2)$$

with $f(0) = 1$ and $f(1) = 1$. Using this definition, we compute $f(2)$ onwards as 2, 3, 5, 8, and so on. Interestingly, for large n, $f(n) \sim a^n$, with a as golden ratio, whose value is $(\sqrt{5}+1)/2$.

The Pingala-Virahanka-Fibonacci sequence have imprints on the growth-related natural patterns (see Figure 35). For example, the numbers of petals in flowers are PVF numbers. Also, the growth of the flowers and shells follow the PVF spiral, which is shown in the first subfigure of Figure 35.

Figure 35: Illustrations of Pingala-Virahanka-Fibonacci sequence and spirals in nature. From https://wikieducator.org/images/f/f1/Fibonacci.png. Credits: wikieducator.

The following recursive code generates the Pingala-Virahanka-Fibonacci sequence:

```
def pingala(n):
    if (n==0):
        return 1
    elif (n==1):
        return 1
    else:
        return (pingala(n-1)+pingala(n-2))
```

Usage:

```
In [5]: pingala(3)
Out[5]: 3
```

```
In [6]: pingala(4)
Out[6]: 5
```

The above examples demonstrate the usefulness of recursive functions.

****

Exercises

1. Show that for Pingala-Virahanka-Fibonacci sequence, $f(n) \sim a^n$ for large n. Compute a.
2. Write a recursive Python function to compute the sum of integers from 1 to n.
3. Write a recursive Python function to compute the product of the elements of an array.
4. Write a recursive Python function that returns the minimum value of an array.

CHAPTER NINE
SOLVING PROBLEMS USING PYTHON

Synopsis

"Any fool can write code that a computer can understand. Good programmers write code that humans can understand." — Martin Fowler

This chapter describes good programming practices, and simple algorithms on prime numbers, searching, and sorting.

9.1 Prime Numbers

Students are quite excited about writing computer programs (also called *codes*). Most of them start to type a program on a computer immediately after a problem is stated. Such hurriedly-written programs are often incorrect. They contain many *bugs* (colloquial word for errors). In the following discussion we provide some tips that you should follow while writing computer programs.

Your objective is to solve a logical problem using a computer. It is you, not the computer, who would solve the problem. A computer is your assistant in this effort. Even though computers can outsmart you on arithmetic operations, they are quite dumb; they need to be told exactly what to do. **Therefore, think clearly about the problem before you start to write a program. Find a solution to the problem at hand. After this, write an algorithm on a piece of paper. After these two steps, you should code.** This way, you would arrive at a correct and error-free code. Rushing to write a computer program leads to a wastage of time and efforts.

I advise you to refer to Chapter Two and see how one discovers solutions to real-life computational problems. In addition, I also advise you to comment your codes. However, avoid commenting excessively.

In this chapter, we will solve several computational problems. For the same, we will write algorithms and then produce Python implementations. We start with several elementary problems related to prime numbers.

Test if an integer is prime or not

There are many clever algorithms to test whether an integer n is prime or not. This is called *primality test*. In this section we will present a simple algorithm for this problem.

Idea: One of the factors of a nonprime number n is always less than equal to $\sqrt{n}$. For example, one of the factors of 21 is 3, which is less than $\sqrt{21}$. Therefore, for primality test, we need to check whether n is divisible by integers from 2 to $\sqrt{n}$. As soon as we find that n is divisible by one of these numbers, we can declare n to be a non-prime. Else, n is a prime.

Algorithm:

```
function is_prime(n):
    for i: 2 to √n
        if (n%i == 0):
            n is non-prime; return
    else  # after the loop
        n is not divisible by any i.
        Declare n to be prime; return
```

Python code:

```
from  numpy import *

# Returns 1 if n is prime, 0 otherwise

def is_prime(n):

    # First test if n is divisible by 2.
    if (n%2 == 0):
        return 0

    # Test if i divides n.
    # i ranges from 3 to sqrt(n) in steps of 2.
    for i in range(3, int(np.sqrt(n))+1, 2):
        if (n%i == 0):
           return 0
    else:
        return 1
```

In the above code, we save computation efforts by skipping the even numbers (i = 2,4,6..) in the loop. If n is indivisible by 2, then it is indivisible by 4 as well. The present program is faster than that in Section 7.3.

Also note that we have imported numpy module using the statement *from numpy import* *; *numpy* is invoked for the *sqrt*() function.

Generating prime numbers up to *n*

For this problem too, we present a simple algorithm called *Sieve of*

Eratosthenes.

Idea: The algorithm has the following steps:

1. Construct a sieve containing all the integers from 2 to *n*.
2. From the sieve eliminate the numbers that are multiples of 2.
3. Do the same for 3, 5, 7, ...
4. Repeat the above process up to $\sqrt{n}$
5. The numbers that remain in the sieve at the end are the desired prime numbers up to *n*.

It is best to test this algorithm for $n = 20$ and 100.

Algorithm: In the algorithm, we remove the non-prime numbers using *pop*() function.

```
function prime_sieve(n):

    Create sieve (2:n)
    prime = prime_no[0]

    loop (prime < sqrt(n))
        for the given prime:
            Eliminate all the multiples of prime
                up to the last number n.
            Retain other numbers.
        Pick the next prime from prime_no.

    The remaining numbers in the sieve are prime numbers.
```

Python code:

```
from  numpy import *

# The function  prime(n) returns a list of primes up to n.
# Adopts the Sieve of Eratosthenes algorithm
# Pops the non-prime numbers from the sieve ones
# a prime is able to divide the number.

def prime(n):

    nos = list(range(2,n+1))
    # Sieve containing integers from 2 to n
```

```
    prime_index = 0
    prime_now = nos[prime_index]
    # First prime

    while (prime_now**2 < n):
        # remove all multiples of prime_now from nos
        index = prime_index + 1

        while (index <= (size(nos)-1)):
            # Loop till the last number in the Sieve
            # if prime_now divides the number,
            # then delete it from the sieve.
            # Otherwise let it be,
            # move on to the next number
            if ((nos[index] % prime_now) != 0):
                index += 1
            else:
                nos.pop(index)

        # Goto the next prime number
        prime_index += 1
        prime_now =  nos[prime_index]
    return nos
```

Usage:

```
In [47]: prime(20)
Out[47]: [2, 3, 5, 7, 11, 13, 17, 19]
```

Compute the prime factors of a number

Finding prime factors is an important problem of number theory. Here, we present a simple algorithm to compute the prime factors of a number.

Idea: We employ the following steps to compute the prime factors of number n.

1. We start with 2. If n is divisible by 2, then 2 is added as a factor, and n is set to $n/2$. We repeat this process until 2 is unable to divide n.

2. We repeat the same process for subsequent prime numbers: 3, 5, 7, …
3. This process is continued till n becomes 1.

Algorithm:

```
prime_no = [2,3,5, …]

function prime_factor(n):
    factor = [] # empty arrays
    i=0
    while (n > 1):
        loop:
            For prime(i),
              if (prime[i] divides n):
                n ← n/prime[i]; Append prime[i] to factor.
        increment i
    return factor
```

Python code:

```
# Prime numbers up to 100
prime_nos = [2, 3, 5, 7, 11, 13, 17, 19, 23, 29, 31, \
37, 41, 43, 47, 53, 59, 61, 67, 71, 73, 79, 83, 89, 97]

# Returns prime factors of integer n
def prime_factor(n):
    factor_array = []
    i = 0
    while (n > 1):
        # loop for prime[i]
        # Inner loop for multiple factors of prime[i]
        while(n%prime_nos[i] == 0):
            n /= prime_nos[i]
            factor_array.append(prime_nos[i])

        # Go to the next prime factor
        i += 1

    return factor_array
```

Usage:

```
In [12]: prime_factor(100)
Out[12]: [2, 2, 5, 5]
```

```
In [15]: prime_factor(17)
Out[15]: [17]
```

With this, we end our discussion on prime numbers.

****

Exercises

1. Consider two integers *a* and *b*. Compute their prime factors. Using these prime factors, write a computer program to compute the greatest common divisor (GCD) and least common multiple (LCM) of *a* and *b*.
2. Find prime factors of the following numbers using a computer program: 24, 95, 4800, 371.
3. Compute GCD of the following set of integers using a computer program: (24,36); (9, 12, 21); (1260,1980)
4. Compute LCD of the following set of integers using a computer program: (24,36); (124,256).
5. *Twin prime numbers* are pair of primes numbers that are separated by 2. Examples of twin primes are (5,7) and (11,13). Write a computer program to compute all the twin prime numbers up to 500.

9.2 *Searching and Sorting*

Searching for an item in a list or in an array is a very important problem. We search for people, things, words, and information all the time. For example, we

1. Search for a word in a dictionary
2. Google search for people, information, etc.
3. Search for a person's image in our brain in order to recognise him/her.

In this section, we present two elementary search algorithms: (a) search in an unsorted array, (b) search in a sorted array. We show that search in a sorted array is faster than that in an unsorted array. We will also present a sort function at the end of the section. Note that a sorted array is one in which the elements are arranged either in increasing or decreasing order.

Searching in an unsorted array

To search for an element x in an unsorted array A, we look for x from the beginning of the array and continue till x is found. This search operation is also called a *linear search* due to the sequential nature of the operation. See Figure 16 for an illustration. Refer to Examples 1 to 5 of Chapter Two for a detailed discussion.

Algorithm:

```
function linsearch(A, x):
    Loop: from the first element to the last element of A.
         Test if A[i] == x; if success, report the index
              and quit the loop.
    else: Report that x is absent in A.
```

Python code:

```
# Searches x in an unsorted array A.
# Returns index i, A[i]=x
```

```
# If x does not belong to A, then return -1
# Linear search
def linsearch(A, x):
    for i in range(len(A)):
        if (A[i] == x):
            return i
    else:  # x does not exist in A
        return -1
```

Usage:

```
In [16] run search.py

In [382]: A = ['Rohit', 'Sita', 'Ahilya', 'Laxmi']

In [383]: linsearch(A, 'Sita')
Out[383]: 1

In [384]: linsearch(A, 'Ahilya')
Out[384]: 2

In [385]: linsearch(A, 'Jaya')
Out[385]: -1
```

How many comparisons are required in the above search operation? If we are lucky, x may be the first element of A. Hence, the best scenario requires a single comparison. In the worst case, x may be at the end of A, in which case we need n comparisons, where n is the size of the array. It is easy to show that on an average, we require $n/2$ comparisons.

Searching in a sorted array

Searching for a number (or an element) in a sorted array is quicker than in an unsorted array. The algorithm makes use of the sorted nature of the array. In the following example, we assume the array A to be sorted in an ascending order.

Idea: We locate the middle element of the array and call it *mid*. If $x = A[mid]$, then done. If $x < A[mid]$, then we search in the left half of the array, else we search in the right half. We continue the above process in the subarray and go on till x is located. Note that this solution is similar to that of Exercise 5 of Chapter Two.

Python code: The following code is based on the above algorithm. The code also takes care of the situations when x does not belong to A.

```
# Search x in an sorted array A.
# Return index i, A[i]=x
# If x does not belong to A, then return -1
# Binary search
def binsearch(A, x):
    n = len(A)
    lower = 0
    upper = n-1
    mid = (lower+upper)//2

    # if x is outside array, return -1
    if ((x < A[0]) | (x>A[-1])):
        return -1

    # If x == A[mid], exit the loop.
    # else, search left or right half depending
    # on x < A[mid] or x>A[mid].
    while (A[mid] != x):
        if (lower == upper):
        # search exhausted.  x not found.
            break
        if (x<A[mid]):
            upper = mid-1
        else:
            lower = mid+1
        mid = (lower+upper)//2

    # Check with the returned mid if A[mid]==x.
    if (A[mid] == x):
        return mid
    else:
        return -1
```

Usage:

```
In [72]: A = [1,3,7,8,11,15,20,25,30]

In [73]: binsearch(A,11)
Out[73]: 4
```

```
In [74]: binsearch(A,35)
Out[74]: -1

In [75]: binsearch(A,9)
Out[75]: -1
```

We illustrate the binary search process in Figure 36. For the array A = [1,3,7,8,11,15,20,25,30], the search process follows the tree diagram illustrated in the figure. First, the program tests if $x == 11$, the middle element. If yes, the program returns the index 4 corresponding to the element "11". Else, the program tests if x<11. If yes, program follows the left branch of the structure, otherwise the program searches for x in the right branch. This procedure is followed at each node. The structure of Figure 36 is called a *tree*. Two branches, which appear at x = 11, bifurcate subsequently into additional sub-branches.

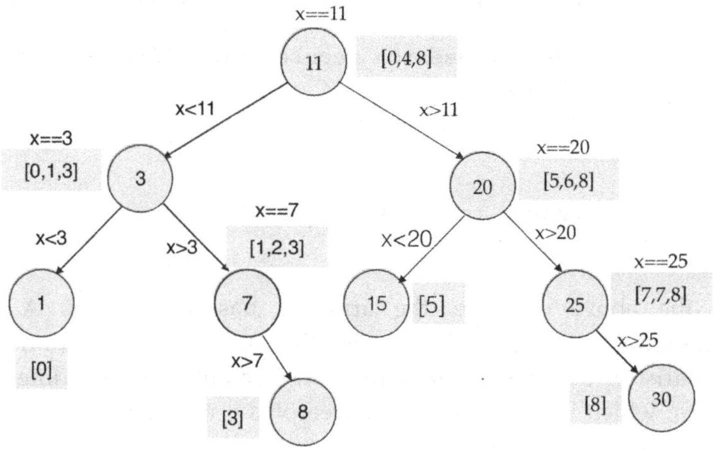

Figure 36: Illustration of a binary search tree for the array A = [1,3,7,8,11,15,20,25,30]. The nodes contain the array elements, while the list in the side is [*lower, mid, upper*]. If *lower* = *upper*, then we list the *middle* element at the node. Note that we start from the middle of the array.

Recursive Python code: The following recursive algorithm provides a more transparent implementation of the binary search. However, the recursive version is more expensive than the non-recursive code described above.

```
# Search x in an sorted array A between A[lower:upper].
# Return index i, A[i]=x
# If x does not belong to A, then return -1
# Recursive binary search
def binsearch_recursive(A,lower,upper,x):

    mid = (lower+upper)/2
    if ((x < A[lower]) | (x>A[upper])):
        return -1
    elif ((lower==upper) & (A[mid] != x)):
        return -1
    else:
        if (A[mid] == x):
            ans = mid
        elif (x < A[mid]):
            ans = binsearch_recursive(A,lower,mid-1,x)
        else:
            ans = binsearch_recursive(A,mid+1,upper,x)
        return ans
```

Usage:

```
In [76]: binsearch_recursive(A,0,8,11)
Out[76]: 4
```

For the above example, the array A has 9 elements. A closer examination of Figure 36 reveals that the maximum number of comparisons required for searching an element is 5 (including ==, <, and >), which is the depth of the tree plus one. We need these many comparisons for $x = 30$.

We can generalise this result to an array of n elements. A binary search for this array will require maximum of $T(n) = (ceil(log_2(n))+1$ comparisons, while the average number of comparisons is $O(log_2(n))$. For large n, $T(n) \ll n/2$. Therefore, we conclude that the binary search is more efficient than the linear search.

In this section, we illustrated search algorithms for an integer list. However, these algorithms are equally applicable to any ordered list. For example, searching a word in language dictionaries is efficient because the dictionaries are sorted. Imagine searching for a word in an unsorted list of words!!

Sorting an array

As described earlier, searching for an element in a sorted array is quicker than in an unsorted array. Hence, sorting an array is an important task in computing. There are many sorting algorithms. Here, we present *bubble sort,* which is the simplest sorting algorithm.

Idea: First, we push the largest element to the top of the array. For the same, we start from beginning of the array and move forward while comparing neighbours. On comparison, if $A[i] > A[i+1]$, we swap the elements. As a result, the largest element reaches the end of A.

After this, we push the second largest number to the end of $A[0{:}N-2]$. Note that this operation is exactly same as the above, except that we perform it on the array $A[0{:}N-2]$. This process is continued till you are left with a single number, which would the smallest number at $A[0]$. The operations described here are observed in bubbling where the lightest element rises to the top.

We illustrate this process in Figure 37. The following code implements the above algorithm.

Python code:

```
# Compare two neighbours: if A[i] < A[i-1], swap.
# In the first round, A[N-1] is the largest integer.
# In the next round, A[N-2] is the second largest number.
# We carry out this process till the end.

# Sort A in increasing order.
def bubble_sort(A):
    n = len(A)

    for i in range(n):
        # A[n-i-1:n-1] is sorted.
        # So go only up to n-i-2.
        for j in range(0, n-i-1):

        # Swap if the prev number is greater
        # than the last number.
```

```
            if A[j] > A[j+1]:
                A[j], A[j+1] = A[j+1], A[j]

In [76]: run bubble_sort.py

In [77]: A = [8,7,3,10,6]

In [78]: bubble_sort(A)

In [79]: A
Out[79]: [3, 6, 7, 8, 10]
```

In Figure 37, we illustrate how the above program sorts array A = [8,7,3,10,6]. In the first iteration (for i = 0 in the loop), the program bubbles the largest integer, which is 10, to the right. In the next iteration, the code bubbles the second largest integer 8. This process is continued till the whole array is sorted.

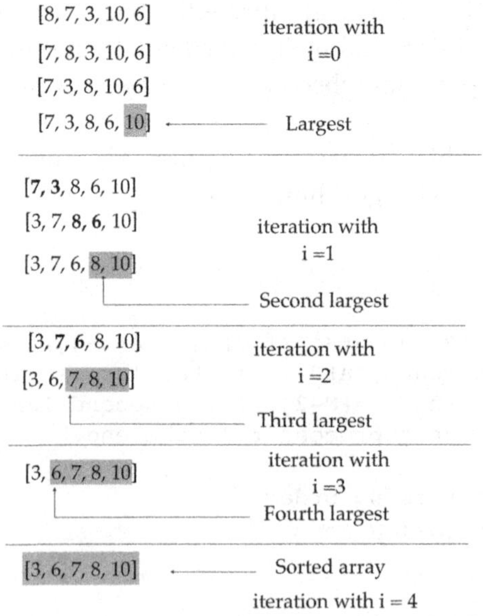

Figure 37: Sorting of array A = [8,7,3,10,6] using bubble sort. The numbers in the shaded regions have been sorted.

With this we end our discussion on search and sort algorithms.

****

Exercises

1. Consider a list of n elements. How many comparisons are required for a linear search in this list? State the number of comparisons for the best-case, worst-case, and average-case scenarios.
2. Consider a list of n sorted elements. How many comparisons are required for a binary search in this array? What is the depth of the search tree? Compare the complexity (number of comparisons) of linear and binary searches for n = 16, 256, 4096, 2^{30}.
3. How many comparisons are required to bubble sort an array of size n?
4. Given an integer array, write a Python function that prints the second largest element of the array.
5. Write a Python function that sorts an array of integers in descending order.
6. Consider a list of strings, for example, A = ["Python", "C", "Java", "Pascal"]. Write a computer program to sort such a list.

Chapter Ten
FILE HANDLING IN PYTHON

Synopsis

"Your memory is a monster; you forget - it doesn't. It simply files things away. It keeps things for you, or hides things from you - and summons them to your recall with a will of its own. You think you have a memory; but it has you!"
— John Irving

In this chapter, we discuss how to save data to a file and how to read data from a file.

10.1 File System

So far, the data for the Python codes were provided in *Ipython* windows. Also, the function *print*() produced an output that appears on the *terminal* (also called *console*). However, such arrangements are impractical for large datasets, which could be the temperatures of all the cities of the world, salaries of the employees of a large company.

Python offers usage of *files* for large datasets. We can read the data from a file or write them into a file. Python offers a wide range of reading and writing options. In this book, we will deal with the simplest of these options—reading and writing text data.

In Python, a file is created by opening a file. For example, a file *f* is created by opening a file *data.txt* using the following Python statement:

```
In [98]: f = open('data.txt', "w")
```

Here, the argument "w" implies that the file is being opened for writing data to the file *f*, which is associated with *data.txt* in the hard disk. The other options for files are listed in Table 8. The append option ("a") is useful for writing data to the file on multiple occasions. The output sent to the file are appended together. The option "r" is used for reading data from a file.

Table 8: Access modes for files

argument	format	Access mode
r	text	read-only
w	text	write
a	text	append
r+	text	read and write
rb	binary	read-only
wb	binary	write
ab	binary	append
rb+	binary	read and write

We also remark that the file *f* is not same as the text tile '*data.txt*' that holds the data. The file *f* contains information about the file size, file type, etc. Also, the data format could be text, binary, or more advanced ones like *Hierarchical Data Formats* (*HDF5*), *Comma Separated Values* (*CSV*). For simplicity, in the present book, we will focus only on text format.

Writing text into a file

You are already familiar with the *print*() function that sends the output to the screen. We can use the same function with an additional argument, *file* = *file_name,* to send the data to the *file_name*. For example, the statement

```
print(x, y, file = f2)
```

sends the variables x and y to file *f2*. This is how we can save the output of a Python program to a file. We can also save double of x and y to the same file using the statement:

```
print(2*x, 2*y, file = f2)
```

Finally we close the file using the statement, *f2.close*(). Let us illustrate the above using the following Python code segment:

```
In [1]: f2 = open('data2.txt', 'a')

In [2]: x=5; y=6

In [3]: print(x, y, file=f2)

In [4]: print(2*x, 2*y, file=f2)

In [5]: f2.close()

In [6]: cat data2.txt
5 6
10 12
```

In the above code segment, the command *cat* lets Python print the contents of the file *data2.txt*.

More commonly used Python functions for writing text to a file are *write*() and *writelines*(), which are used for writing a string and set of lines respectively. We illustrate these functions using Python statements given below:

```
In [100]: f = open('data.txt', "w")

In [101]: f.write("Hi! \n")
Out[101]: 5

In [102]: str_list = ["This is month of June. \n", "It is
very hot here. \n", "Expect rains next month. \n"]

In [103]: f.writelines(str_list)  # write lines of text

In [104]: f.close()

In [105]: cat data.txt
Hi!
This is month of June.
It is very hot here.
Expect rains next month.
```

Reading text from a file

We an also read data from a file. For the same, we employ the following steps:

1. Open the file using "r" or "r+" option.
2. The file pointer is set to the zeroth byte of the file.
3. The function *f.readline*() is used for reading the current line of the file (*f*).
4. The function *f.read*() is used to read the file contents from current position to the end of file (EOF).
5. We can reset the file pointer to the *n*th byte using *f.seek*(*n*). The function f.seek(0) takes the file pointer to the beginning of the file.
6. Python statement *for line in f*: is a convenient way to read a file line by line.

We illustrate the above Python functions using the following code segment. We read the *'data.txt'* file that was generated earlier.

```
In [127]: f = open('data.txt', "r+")
```

```
In [128]: print(f.readline())
     ...: print(f.readline())
Hi!

This is month of June.

In [129]: print(f.read())
It is very hot here.
Expect rains next month.

In [130]: f.seek(0)
Out[130]: 0

In [131]: str_read = f.read()

In [132]: str_read
Out[132]: 'Hi! \nThis is month of June. \nIt is very hot
here. \nExpect rains next month. \n'

In [133]: f.seek(0)
Out[133]: 0

In [134]: for line in f:
     ...:     print(line, end='')
     ...:
Hi!
This is month of June.
It is very hot here.
Expect rains next month.
```

Next, we show how to read/write a numpy array to a file.

Input/Output of Numpy arrays to a file

Python offers functions for reading and writing Numpy arrays. Python's *numpy module* offers functions *save*() and *savetxt*() to save an array into a file, and *load*() and *loadtxt*() to load an array to the memory from a txt file. We illustrate these functions using the following code segment.

```
import numpy as np
x = np.arange(0,2*np.pi,0.01)
y = np.cos(x)
```

```
np.save('data_x.npy', x)
np.save('data_y.npy', y)
x_read_txt = np.load('data_x.npy')
y_read_txt = np.load('data_y.npy')

np.savetxt('data_x.txt', x)
np.savetxt('data_y.txt', y)
x_read_txt2 = np.loadtxt('data_x.txt')
y_read_txt2 = np.loadtxt('data_y.txt')
```

The functions *save*() and *load*() work with *.npy* files, while *savetxt*() and *loadtxt*() work with *.txt* files. Note that, by default, the text data is saved in exponential format. We could save the data in float format with finite precision (here, up to 3 decimal places) as follows.

```
np.savetxt("month.txt", month, fmt="%0.3f", delimiter=",")
```

The above discussion illustrates how we can use Python to read data from a file and write in a file. Python offers many more input/output features, for example, reading and writing compressed data or binary data. These discussions, however, are beyond the scope of this book.

****

Exercises

1. Write a Python code to print integers 1 to 100 in a file '*number.txt*'. After the writing operation, read the numbers back into the computer and assign it to an array named *number*.
2. Write your name in a file, '*name.txt*'. Write a Python code to read this file and assign its contents to a string named *your_name*.

Part Three

School Maths using Python

"Without mathematics, there's nothing you can do. Everything around you is mathematics. Everything around you is numbers." — Shakuntala Devi

Chapter Eleven
ALGEBRA USING PYTHON

Synopsis

"An equation means nothing to me unless it expresses a thought of God."
— Srinivas Ramanujan

This chapter introduces usage of Python in algebra, trigonometry, and plotting.

11.1 Algebra and Trigonometry using Python

Python's Numpy library has many mathematical functions that can help us master school mathematics. We introduce some important functions that you encounter in school algebra and in trigonometry.

The *power* operator in python is ** and, its inverse operator is *logarithm*. For example,

$2^x = y$ and $log_2(y) = x$;
$10^x = y$ and $log_{10}(y) = x$;
$e^x = y$ and $log(y) = x$

In general, if $y = f(x)$, then the inverse f^{-1} obeys the following property: $x = f^{-1}(y)$.

Logarithm and exponentiation are functions of Numpy library, which is included in *pylab*. We illustrate their usage using the following Python statements:

```
In [2]: 2**6
Out[2]: 64

In [3]: log2(64)
Out[3]: 6.0

In [4]: 10**0.6
Out[4]: 3.9810717055349722

In [5]: log10(Out[4])    # Out[4] =  3.9810717055349722
Out[5]: 0.6

In [6]: exp(5)
Out[6]: 148.4131591025766

In [7]: log(Out[6])
Out[7]: 5.0
```

Python can help us learn trigonometry as well. All the trigonometric functions are part of Numpy. The arguments of trigonometric functions are in *radians*, and the inverse of *sin*() and *cos*() are *arcsin*()

and *arccos*() respectively.

```
In [24]: sin(pi/2)
Out[24]: 1.0

In [25]: sin(pi/10)
Out[25]: 0.3090169943749474

In [26]: arcsin(Out[25])      # inverse(sin)
Out[26]: 0.3141592653589793  # pi

In [27]: tan(pi/4)
Out[27]: 0.9999999999999999
```

We can sum a series using Python. In fact, Python computes many functions, including trigonometric and logarithm, by summing up their series expressions. Note, however, that the series employed by Python may be more sophisticated than what are listed in your textbooks. Here we compute *sin*(x) using a series sum, which is,

$$\sin(x) = \sum_{k=0}^{\infty} (-1)^k \frac{x^{2k+1}}{(2k+1)!} = x - \frac{x^3}{3!} + \frac{x^5}{5!} + \ldots$$

Since we can not perform an infinite sum in a computer, and we terminate the series at some level. The following Python function sums the series up to n terms.

```
import math

def my_sin(x, n):
    sum = x
    for k in range(1,n):
        sum = sum + (-1)**(k)*x**(2*k+1)/
                 math.factorial(2*k+1)
    return (sum)
```

Note that *factorial*(), which is a function of *math* library, is invoked using *math.factorial*(). We test our function by computing *sin*($\pi/4$) for n = 5 and 10 and compare the results with the actual value.

```
In [13]: my_sin(pi/4,5)
Out[13]: 0.7071067829368671
```

```
In [14]: my_sin(pi/4,10)
Out[14]: 0.7071067811865475

In [15]: sin(pi/4)
Out[15]: 0.7071067811865475
```

For $x = \pi/4$, the results for $n = 5$ and 10 are accurate up to 8 and 16 digits respectively. Clearly, the above series solution for sin(x) is quite accurate.

Using similar computation, we can evaluate *exp*(x), whose series expansion is

$$e^x = \sum_{k=0}^{\infty} \frac{x^k}{k!} = 1 + x + \frac{x^2}{2!} + \frac{x^3}{3!} + \frac{x^4}{4!} + \ldots$$

An implementation of the function *exp*(x,n) is given below:

```
def my_exp(x, n):
    sum = 1+x
    for k in range(2,n+1):
        sum = sum + x**k/math.factorial(k)
        print (k, sum)
    return sum
```

We test the above code at $x = 1$ for $n = 5$ and 10.

```
In [38]: my_exp(1,5)
Out[38]: 2.7166666666666663

In [39]: my_exp(1,10)
Out[39]: 2.7182818011463845

In [40]: exp(1)
Out[40]: 2.718281828459045
```

The series sum for $n = 5$ and 10 provides accurate results up to 3 and 8 significant digits respectively, which are far worse than the results for *sin*(x). This is because the series convergence of *exp*(x) is quite slow. Compare this convergence with that for *sin*(x)! In fact, sophisticated algorithms are employed to compute *exp*(x).

Example 1: In this example we illustrate a sophisticated series solution. Ramanujan showed that π can be computed quite accurately using the following series (reference: wikipedia.org).

$$\frac{1}{\pi} = \frac{2\sqrt{2}}{9801} \sum_{k=0}^{\infty} \frac{(4k)!(1103 + 26390k)}{(k!)^4 396^{4k}}$$

The following Python code computes π by summing the first n terms of above series.

```
import math
sum = 1103

n=3
for k in range(1,n):
    sum = sum + math.factorial(4*k)*(1103+2030*k)/
(math.factorial(k)**4 * 396**(4*k))

sum = sum * 2*sqrt(2)/9801
approx_pi = 1/sum
print (approx_pi)
```

For the first three terms, the above code yields $\pi = 3.1415927213043657$, which is accurate up to 7 significant digits (actual value of π = 3.141592653589793...).

Many more things can be done using Python. In Section *9.1* we described simple algorithms related to prime numbers. One can also dig deeper into other aspects of number theory. As discussed in *Chapter Three* and *Chapter Four,* we can learn about various number system using Python. There is also interesting mathematics behind how numbers are stored inside a computer. These complex topics are covered in college books.

In addition, using *Symbolic Python* (*sympy*), we can also prove trigonometric identities. Unfortunately we cannot discuss *sympy* in this introductory book. However, we encourage the interested students to browse through some examples of *sympy* functions on the website https://www.sympy.org/

****

Exercises

1. What are the inverse functions of *sin*(x), *exp*(x), *log*(x), *tan*(x), x^2, x^3, x^n, and 7^x? Verify these functions by evaluating them in Python for appropriate arguments.
2. For $\theta = 35$ degrees, compute $\sin\theta$, $(\tan\theta)^4$, $\sin^2\theta+\cos^2\theta$, $\sin 2\theta$ using Python.
3. Find the solution of the equation $\sin\theta = \theta/2$ by iterating $\theta_{n+1} = 2\sin(\theta_n)$. Choose θ_0 near 2.
4. Compute *cos*(x) and *tan*(x) using series solution. Test the accuracy of your series solution.
5. Which is larger, e^{π} or π^e?
6. For triangles, test the following trigonometric identities numerically using Python. That is, show that the identities hold for several triangles. Refer to the figure shown below for the definitions of various symbols.

$$\frac{\sin A}{a} = \frac{\sin B}{b} = \frac{\sin C}{c}$$

$$\cos A = \frac{b^2 + c^2 - a^2}{2ab}$$

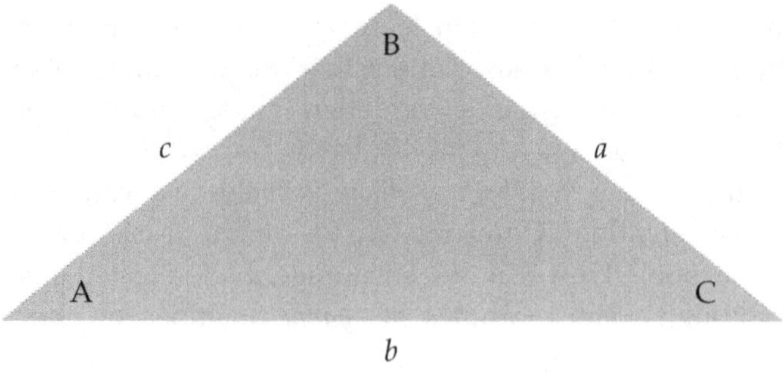

11.2 Plotting in Python

Computer programs, experiments, and observations create data. Python is used extensively for analysis and visualization of such data. In this chapter we describe how to plot the data in Python.

Let us revisit the monthly temperature data discussed in Section 6.3. We can plot the data using the following plot commands:

```
In [1]: month = linspace(1,12,12)

In [2]: temperature = array([5, 9, 15, 20, 35, 40, 39, 34,
27, 22, 10, 9])

In [3]: plot(month, temperature,  'bo-')
Out[3]: [<matplotlib.lines.Line2D at 0x1267066d0>]
```

The plot function makes a plot of *month* vs. *temperature,* with *month* and *temperature* along the x and y axes respectively. The argument 'bo-' instructs Python that the curve is of blue (b) color with data at the dots (o), and that the data points are to be joined by a solid curve (-). If you want to make a plot without lines, replace 'bo-' with 'bo'. For a dashed line, replace 'bo-' with 'bo--'. We label the x and y axes of the plots as *'Month'* and *'Temperature'* respectively using the following statements. The function *grid*() puts a grid in the figure. See Figure 38 for the plots.

```
In [4]: xlabel('Month')
Out[4]: Text(0.5, 47.04444444444444, 'Month')

In [5]: ylabel('Temperature')
Out[5]: Text(93.94444444444443, 0.5, 'Temperature')

In [6]: grid()
```

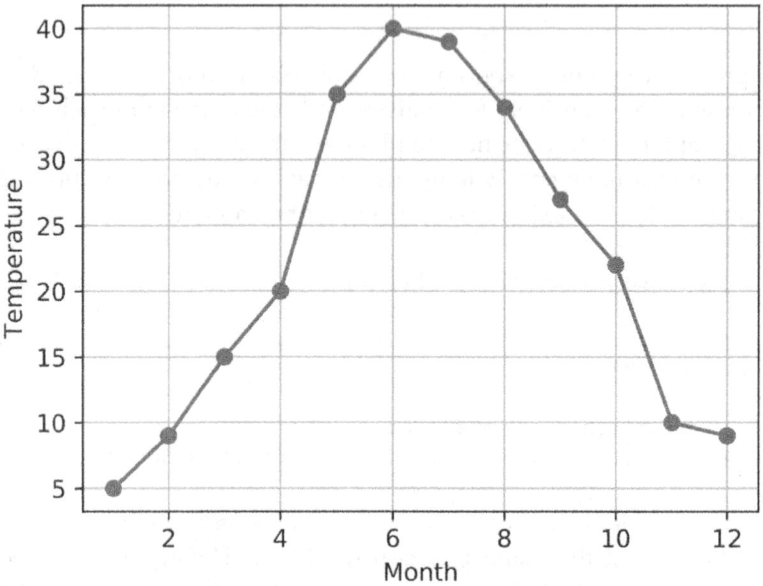

Figure 38: Plot of city temperature for various months.

The plot pops up in a separate window with the following panel at the bottom. We can control the plot using the commands of the panel.

The functions of the buttons (taken from matplotlib.org) are as follows:

 (Zoom-to-rectangle): We can zoom into a subregion (a rectangle) of the plot.

 (Pan/Zoom): We can move the plot using mouse. It also displays the x and y coordinates of the cursor position.

 (Save): We can save the figure in a file. The allowed formats are

pdf, png, svg, ps, and *eps*. I recommend using *pdf* or *png* formats.

 (Home, Forward, and Back): *Home* button reverts to the original configuration. The *left* and *right* arrows help navigate back and forth between previously defined views.

Figure 38 was saved using the above function of the menu bar. In the following examples, we illustrate more features of the plot function.

Example 1: Let us plot the function $y = x^2$. For the same we sample 100 points for x in the interval [0,2], and then compute $y = x^2$. After this we plot x vs. y using the following code segment. The resulting plot is illustrated in Figure 39.

```
In [114]: x=linspace(0,2,100)

In [115]: y=x**2

In [116]: plot(x,y); xlabel('x'); ylabel(‘y’)
Out[116]: Text(0, 0.5, 'y(x)')

In [117]: xlim([0,2]); ylim([0,4]);  grid();

# xlim and ylim limit the ranges of x and y axes.
```

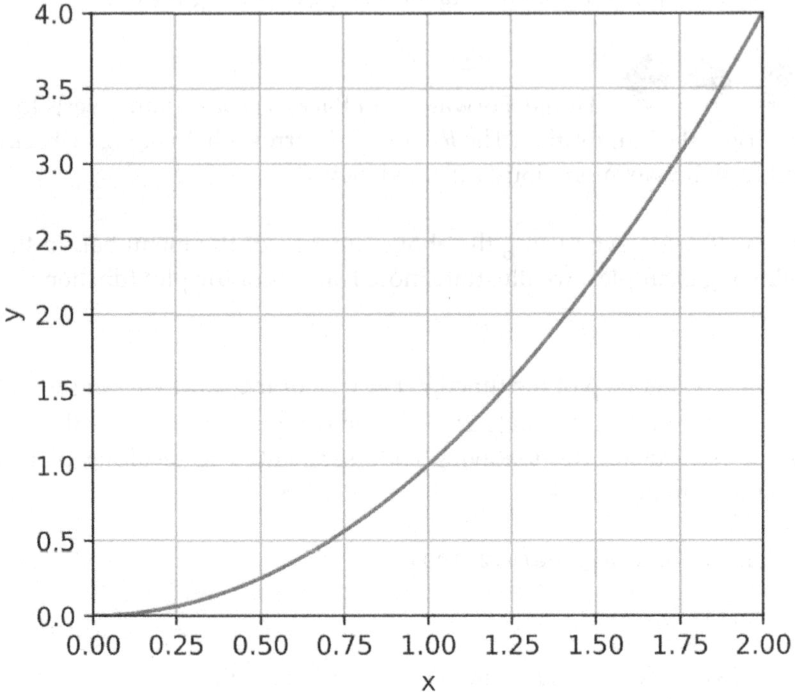

Figure 39: Plot of $y=x^2$.

Example 2: We plot $sin(x)$ and x/2 in Figure 40. The curves intersect at two points, $x = 0$ and near $x = 2.0$. We can determine the intersection point by iterating $x_{n+1} = 2\ sin(x_n)$ starting from $x_0 = 2.0$. The code used to make the plots is given below.

```
x = linspace(0,pi,100)
plot(x, sin(x))
plot(x, x/2)

xlim(0,pi)
ylim(0,1.5)
xlabel('x')
grid()
```

Example 3: In Figure 41, we exhibit a plot of $log(x)$ that exhibits the slow growth of the function. As shown in the figure, we can get the coordinate (x,y) using the pan/zoom symbol at the menu bar. The coordinate of the tip of the cursor (shown as a short arrow) is (x,y) = (2.00101, 0.671018). The code used to make the plots is as follows:

```
x = linspace(0.1,5,100)
plot(x, log(x))
xlim(0,5); ylim(-2.5,1.7)
xlabel('x'); ylabel('log(x)'); grid()
```

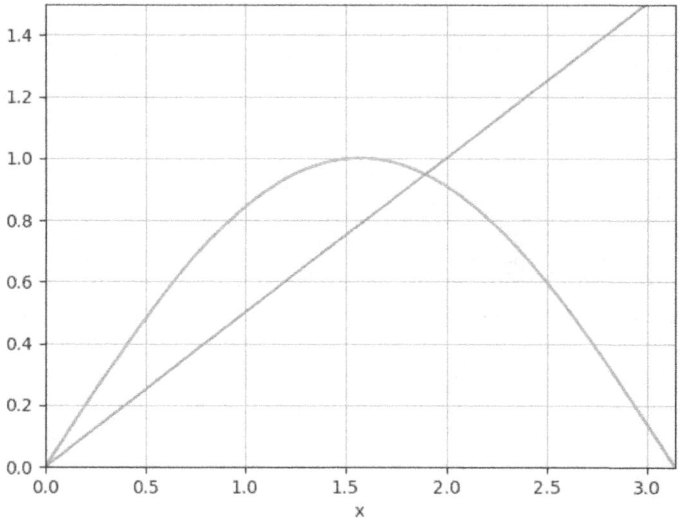

Figure 40: Plots of y=$sin(x)$ (orange curve) and $x/2$ (green straight line).

Example 4: Figure 42 exhibits a plot of $exp(x)$ that grows much faster than $log(x)$. The code used to make the plots is as follows:

```
x = linspace(0,5,100)
plot(x, exp(x))
xlim(0,5); ylim(0,150)
xlabel('x'); ylabel('exp(x)'); grid()
```

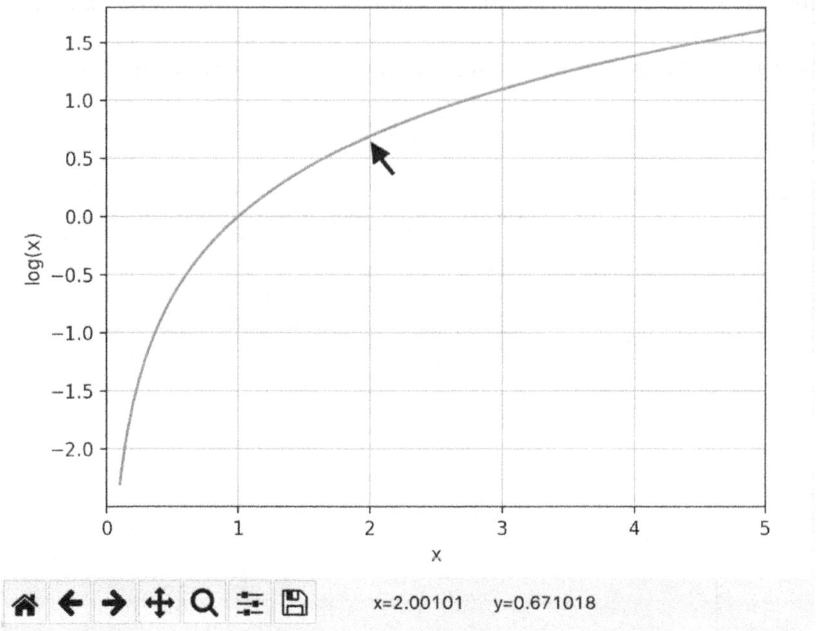

Figure 41: Plot of y=log(x).

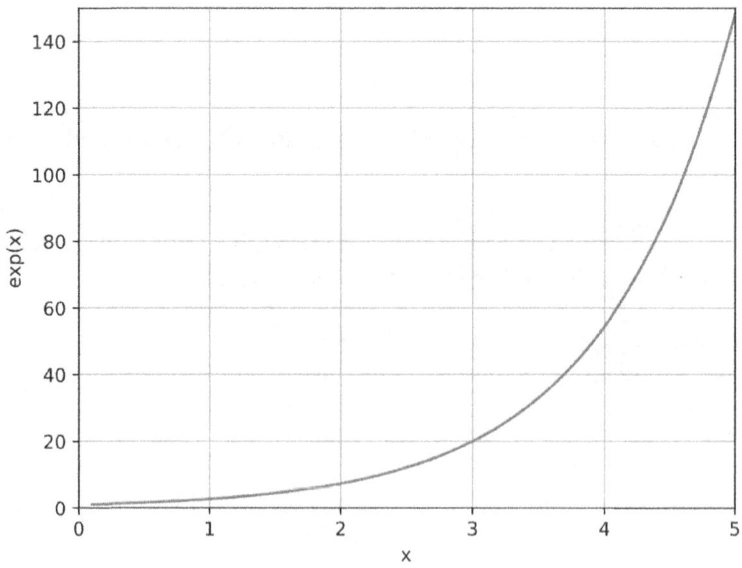

Figure 42: Plot of y= exp(x).

Python offers many functions for making complex plots. However, these topics are beyond the scope of this book.

****

Exercises

1. Plot x vs. $cos(x)$ in the range $(0,2\pi)$. Also plot x vs. $cos^2(x)$ in the same figure. Save the figure as test.pdf.
2. Download the year-wise population of India. Make a plot of it and save it as india_population.png. Download the population data for India from https://www.worldometers.info/world-population/india-population/.
3. Plot the following functions as a function of x: $\sqrt{x}$, x^2, x^3, x^4, x^5, x^{10}.
4. Plot x vs. $log(x^2)$, as well x vs. $e^{x/3}$, in the range $x = [0.1,5]$.
5. Plot the trajectory of a projectile that is shot with velocity of 10 m/s at an angle of 45 degrees from the horizontal. Ignore air friction.

CHAPTER TWELVE

GEOMETRY USING PYTHON

Synopsis

"There is geometry in the humming of the strings, there is music in the spacing of the spheres." — Pythagorus

In this chapter, we will focus on how to learn geometry and programming using Python's Turtle module.

12.1 Geometry Using Turtle

The python module *Turtle* can help us learn school-level geometry, as well as computer programming. In this section, we will illustrate how to draw various geometrical patterns using the *Turtle* module.

In this setup, a turtle, who is very patient and obedient, follows the exact instructions given to her. It could move forward by a distance d (*forward*(d)), turn left by any angle θ (*left*(θ)), turn right by an angle ζ (*right*(ζ)), go to a point (x,y) (*goto*(x,y)), and perform several other tasks. We illustrate these moves in Figure 43.

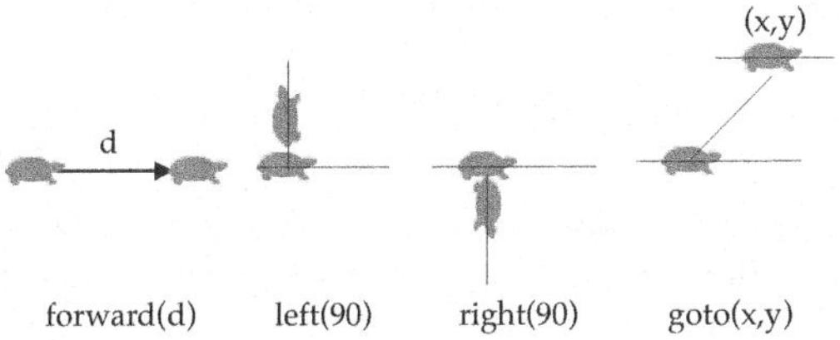

Figure 43: Movements of the turtle on various commands.

Python commands *penup*() and *pendown*() are used for transferring the turtle to a new point without drawing a line. For example, if we want the turtle to start drawing from point (a,b), we issue the following commands to the turtle:

```
turtle.penup()
turtle.goto(a,b)
turtle.pendown()
```

Turtle movements are possible on a graphic window, called *console*. Unfortunately, we cannot create a console in an *ipython* terminal. However, we can do so using a graphical user interface (GUI) provided by *Spyder*. Refer to Section Python in your machine for an introduction to *Spyder*. In the *ipython* console of *Spyder*, we can type instructions for the turtle. The movements of the turtle will appear in a separate console, *Python Turtle Graphics,* which is illustrated in Figure 44.

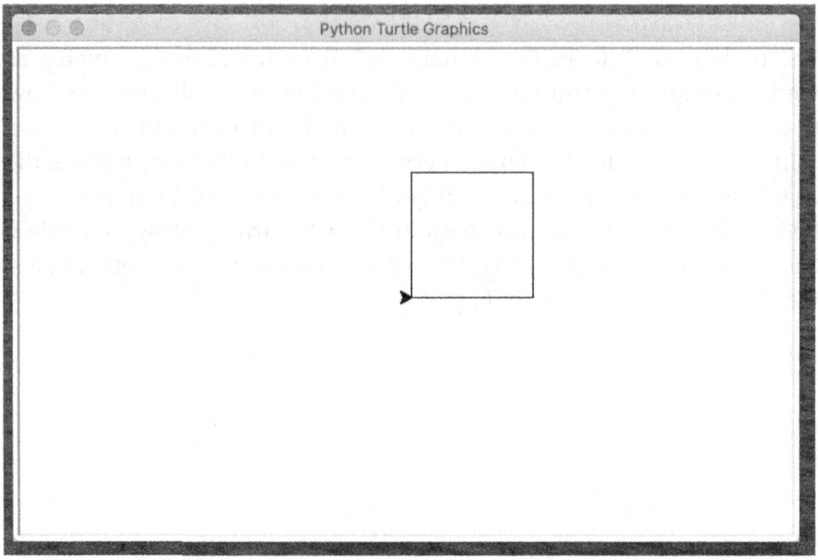

Figure 44: The turtle console displaying a square drawn by the turtle.

We start the *Turtle* module using the following command:

import turtle

After this, we can write turtle commands in the editor console and execute them using the ▶ command in the GUI. For example, the following set of commands

```
turtle.forward(100)
turtle.left(120)
turtle.forward(100)
turtle.left(120)
turtle.forward(100)
turtle.left(120)
```

creates an equilateral triangle whose sides are 100 units long (see Figure 45(a)). Note that we can also construct the same triangle using the following loop:

```
for i in range(3):
    turtle.forward(100)
```

```
    turtle.left(120)
```

In the figure, the turtle is represented by an arrowhead. The turtle comes back to the original configuration after the loop. We can also construct a square and a hexagon by making the turtle turn by angles 90 and 60 degrees respectively (see Figure 45(b,c)).

Note that if the turtle turns left by 125 degrees at each forward movement, it will never return to its original position. Hence, we cannot form a closed figure by making the turtle turn by 125 degrees. The following code produces Figure 45(d) after 100 iterations.

```
for i in range(100):
    turtle.forward(100)
    turtle.left(125)
```

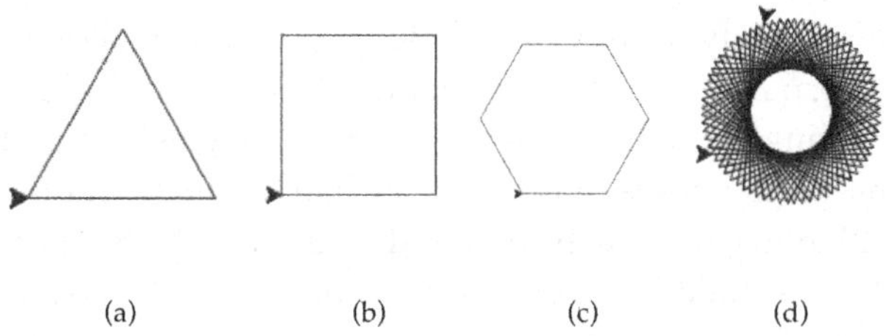

Figure 45: Turtle's creation: (a) a triangle, (b) a square, (c) a hexagon (d) non-closing pattern for turn of 125 degrees.

The turtle can also draw a circle of radius r under the following command (See Figure 46(a)):

```
r = 25
turtle.circle(r)
```

Under the command, *turtle.circle*(r,θ), the turtle draws a circular arc of radius r and spanning angle θ. We can use the above command to draw a spiral shown in Figure 46(b).

```
r = 25
for i in range(96):
```

```
    t.circle(r + i, 22.5)
```

Note that in the loop, the radius of the arc increases after each iteration.

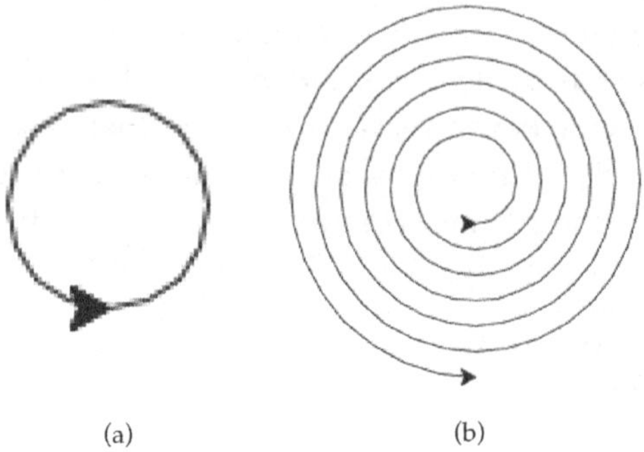

Figure 46: (a) A circle and (b) a spiral produced by the turtle.

Now we are ready to draw a complex figure called *Sierpinski triangle,* which is shown in Figure 47. This triangle has fractal degree of 3. Note that each triangle (parent) has three sub-triangles (daughters). The dimensions of the three daughters is half of their parent (see, for example, blue triangle within a red triangle). Note that the sub-triangles have smaller triangles within them. The recursive iteration, however, stops at the innermost green triangles. We represent a triangle with its degree. If the depth of a triangle is n, then those of its sub-triangles are $n-1$. In Figure 47, the *fractal degrees* of white, blue, green, and red triangles are 3, 2, 1, 0 respectively. Based on these observations, an algorithm to construct Sirpiński triangle is as follows.

```
def draw_sirpinski(vertex_coords, fractal_degree):

     Draw a triangle of fractal_degree.

     if (fractal_degree > 0):
         Find the coordinates of the triangle
              at the left corner
         draw_sirpinski(left_triange_vertex_coords,
              fractal_degree-1)

         Find the coordinates of the triangle at
              the right corner
         draw_sirpinski(right_triagle_vertex_coords,
```

```
            fractal_degree-1)

        Find the coordinates of the triangle at
            the top corner
        draw_sirpinski(top_triangle_vortex_coords,
            fractal_degree-1)
```

Figure 47: Sierpinski triangle of degree 3 created by Turtle. This is a black-white version of the coloured figure, which is hosted on https://sites.google.com/view/py-school.

The code that produces the Sierpinski triangle with fractal degree of fractal_degree is given below:

```
import turtle

colormap = ['red','green','blue',
'white','yellow','violet','orange']

# Draws a triangle of color 'color' and whose vortices are
in the list vortex_coords.
def drawTriangle(vortex_coords,color,fractalTurtle):
    fractalTurtle.fillcolor(color)
    fractalTurtle.up()
    fractalTurtle.goto(vortex_coords[0][0],
        vortex_coords[0][1])
    fractalTurtle.down()
    fractalTurtle.begin_fill()
    fractalTurtle.goto(vortex_coords[1][0],
        vortex_coords[1][1])
    fractalTurtle.goto(vortex_coords[2][0],
        vortex_coords[2][1])
    fractalTurtle.goto(vortex_coords[0][0],
```

```
        vortex_coords[0][1])
    fractalTurtle.end_fill()

# Returns the mid point of points p1 and p2
def mid_point(p1,p2):
    return ((p1[0]+p2[0])/2, (p1[1]+p2[1])/2)

# Draws sierpinski triangle of fractal_degree with its
def
sierpinski(vortex_coords,fractal_degree,fractalTurtle):
   drawTriangle(vortex_coords, colormap[fractal_degree],
               fractalTurtle)
    if fractal_degree > 0:
       sierpinski([vortex_coords[0],
          mid_point(vortex_coords[0], vortex_coords[1]),
          mid_point(vortex_coords[0], vortex_coords[2])],
          fractal_degree-1, fractalTurtle)

       sierpinski([vortex_coords[1],
          mid_point(vortex_coords[0], vortex_coords[1]),
          mid_point(vortex_coords[1], vortex_coords[2])],
          fractal_degree-1, fractalTurtle)

       sierpinski([vortex_coords[2],
          mid_point(vortex_coords[2],vortex_coords[1]),
          mid_point(vortex_coords[0],vortex_coords[2])],
          fractal_degree-1, fractalTurtle)

def main():
   fractalTurtle = turtle.Turtle()
   Win = turtle.getscreen()
   vortex_coords = [[-200,-100],[0,200],[200,-100]]
   sierpinski(vortex_coords,3,fractalTurtle)
   Win.exitonclick()

main()
```

The above code is self explanatory. Here we list some of the key features of the code.

1. The above code is recursive (see Section *8.2*).
2. The functions *sierpinski*() and *drawTriangle*() need the *fractalTurtle* as an argument because the same turtle executes these functions. Therefore, in *main*(), we create *fractalTurtle* using the function *turtle.Turtle*(); this *fractalTurtle* is passed as

an argument to all the relevant functions.

3. The colors of the triangles depend on their degrees. Based on the *colormap* = [], the triangles of levels 3, 2, 1, 0 have white, blue, green, and red colors respectively. Note that level n triangles are drawn on top of level $n-1$ triangles, hence only the remnants of the earlier triangles are visible in the figure. The colors of the Sierpinski triangle are not pure colors due to the overlapping regions.
4. The centre of the largest triangle is at the origin, while its three vortices are at (–200,–100), (0,200), (200,–100), which is in the array *vortex_coords*. The vortices of the inner triangles are computed iteratively.
5. The color-filling of the triangles is achieved by the functions *fillcolor*(), *begin_fill*(), and *end_fill*(). Note that a triangle is drawn first, and then it is filled with color.

With this we close our discussion on turtle package of Python. You can refer to Python documentation *https://docs.python.org/2/library/turtle.html* for more details.

As you may have observed, we can learn programming structure of Python (discussed in *Chapter Seven* and *Chapter Eight*) using the *turtle* module.

****

Exercises

Construct the following figures using the *turtle* module:

1. A right-angled triangle whose sides are 30, 40, and 50 units.
2. An isosceles triangle whose sides are 20, 30, and 30 units.
3. A rectangle whose sides are 100, 50, 100, and 50 units.
4. A regular hexagon whose sides are 120 units long.
5. A regular pentagon whose sides are 100 units long.
6. A regular octagon whose sides are 100 units long.
7. A cube whose edges are 100 unit long.
8. A tetrahedron whose edges are 100 unit long.
9. A simple house.
10. A tree

12.2 Coordinate Geometry Using Turtle

Coordinate geometry is a difficult subject. Turtle programming can make Coordinate geometry fun. Some important points in this topic are

1. The centre of the turtle canvas is at the origin, which is $x = 0$, $y = 0$.
2. The turtle can be asked to move to any point from its current location. The command *goto*(x,y) takes the turtle to a point with coordinates (x,y).
3. Interestingly, the turtle does not reorient itself under the *goto* operation. This is unlike combined operation of *left*(θ) and *forward*(d), in which the turtle turns left by an angle θ.

In the following example, the turtle makes an isosceles triangle whose vortices are located at coordinates (0,0), (200,0), and (100,100).

```
import turtle

t = turtle.Turtle()
myWin = turtle.getscreen()

t.goto(200,0)
t.goto(100,100)
t.goto(0,0)
```

The turtle draws the isosceles triangle shown in Figure 48(a). A minor change in the above script makes the turtle draw a right-angled triangle whose vortices are located at (0,0), (200,0), and (0,100). See Figure 48(b) for an illustration.

```
t.goto(200,0)
t.goto(0,100)
t.goto(0,0)
```

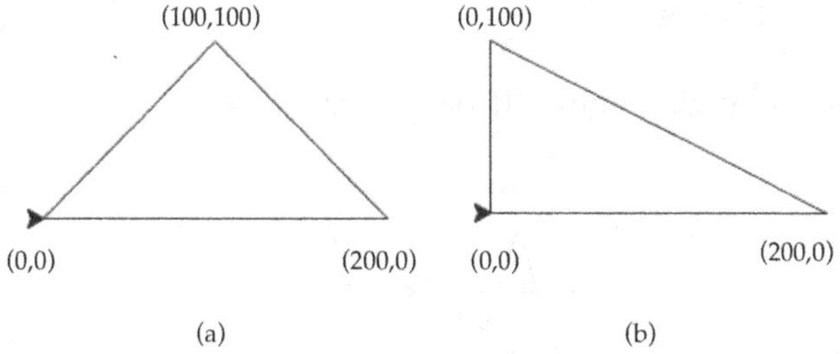

Figure 48: Turtle's creation: (a) An isosceles triangle. (b) A right-angled triangle.

We can construct more complex figures using the *Turtle* module. For example, we can ask the turtle to draw a house once we know the coordinates of the corners of the house.

We point out that there are many apps for computers, mobiles, and tablets that can help you learn geometry and coordinate geometry. Some of the popular android apps on geometry can be found at https://appgrooves.com/rank/education/geometry/best-apps-for-learning-geometry.

With this we close our discussion on how to learn geometry using Python.

****

Exercises

Construct the following figures using the *goto*(x,y) command of the *Turtle* module:

1. A right-angled triangle whose sides are 30, 40, and 50 units.
2. An triangle whose vortices are at (100,0), (190,0), (150,70).
3. A rectangle whose vortices are at (0,0), (190,30), (150,70), (0,100).

4. A square of side 100 units starting from (0,0) and moving to (100,0).
5. A simple house.
6. A tree
7. The following figures (from *wikipedia.org*):

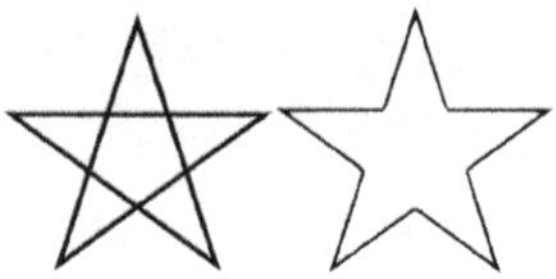

CHAPTER THIRTEEN
MACHINE LEARNING

Synopsis

"AI is one of the most important things humanity is working on. It is more profound than, I dunno, electricity or fire." — Sundar Pichai, Google CEO.

This chapter provides a brief introduction to statistics and machine learning.

13.1 Linear Regression

Machine Learning (ML) is one of the most important topics of science. The Chief Executive Officer (CEO) of Google, Sundar Pichai, believes that ML is one of the most important things humanity is working on. This topic is very broad and complex, hence we cannot cover it in this introductory book. In this section, we will give a very broad overview of regression-based ML, which is one of the important methods. But, before that, we will briefly cover basics of statistics.

Statistical analysis

Many variables in the world are random. For example, the heights of men and women are random (around a mean). If we sample 10 men, their heights in centimetres could be 160, 170, 175, 165, 173, 163, 180, 163, 172. For a large sample size, it is impossible to list heights of all the men in books or reports. Rather, it is sensible to describe the data using *mean, standard deviation,* and *median,* which are defined below:

Mean: For a variable x, the *mean* $<x>$, is defined as an average over the data sample. Note that the angular brackets have been used to denote the mean value. For n data points, we sum over the data and divide the sum by n. That is,

$$< x > = \frac{\sum x}{n}.$$

Standard deviation: The standard deviation of a set of numbers is a measure of the dispersion of the data. This quantity, denoted by $std(x)$, is

$$\text{std}(x) = \sqrt{< x^2 >} = \left(\frac{\sum x^2}{n}\right)^{1/2}.$$

Median: The median of a set of numbers is the middle number of its sorted list (ascending or descending).

```
In [23]: x = array([160, 170, 175, 165, 173, 163, 180,
163, 172])

In [24]: mean(x)
Out[24]: 169.0

In [26]: sum(x)/9
Out[26]: 169.0

In [22]: sort(x)
Out[22]: array([160, 163, 163, 165, 170, 172, 173, 175,
180])

In [21]: median(x)
Out[21]: 170.0

In [28]: std(x)
Out[28]: 6.253887679764573

In [27]: y = x - mean(x)

In [29]: sqrt(sum(y**2)/9)
Out[29]: 6.253887679764573
```

After this basic introduction of statistics, we introduce *linear regression*.

Linear regression

Let us consider an example. It has been observed that the weight of a healthy individual is proportional to his/her height. See Figure 49 for an illustration. The dots in the figure represent the sample. That is, each dot represents height and weight of an individual. Clearly, the dots are scattered. However, one can easily guess that weight (W) is proportional to height (H). This linear relation can be obtained using linear regression as follows.

Let us denote the height and weight of ith individual by W_i and H_i respectively, and present it as a point (W_i, H_i) in the plot. We postulate a relation between these variables as

$$W = aH + b$$

with a and b as unknown constants. As shown in the figure, many data points do not lie on the linear curve, hence the function $W = aH + b$ is only an approximate or guessed relationship, not an exact one. We derive the constants a and b by minimising the following error function:

$$\text{Error} = \sum (W_i - a\,H_i - b)^2$$

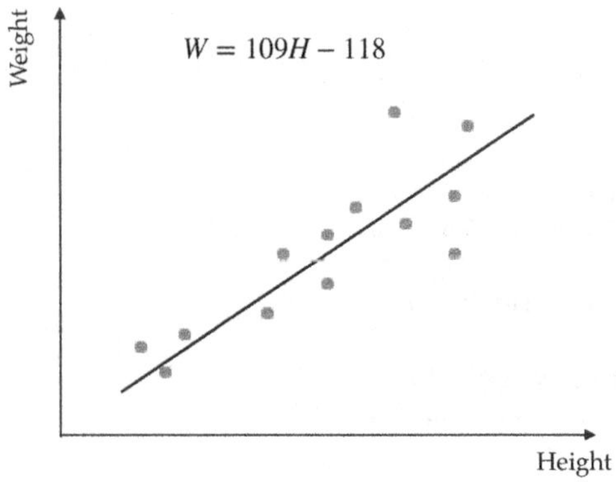

Figure 49: Plot of *height* vs. *weight* for healthy human beings. The dots represent the sample data, and the straight line in the middle is the best-fit curve obtained using linear regression.

This minimisation procedure is somewhat complex. Here, we state the formulas for a and b derived using the error-minimisation procedure:

$$a = \frac{< WH > - < W > < H >}{< H^2 > - < H >^2}$$

$$b = < W > - a < H >$$

Thus, we determine the desired approximate relationship $W = aH + b$, which is a straight line. This curve is called *best-fit curve,* which is illustrated as the black line in Figure 49. The procedure is called *linear regression*. Given the data W and H in two linear arrays, the Python function *polyfit*() yields a and b. We will describe the usage of *polyfit* function below.

Once the regression function is known, we can estimate the weight of a healthy human of height H. An example of such a function is $W = 109\ H - 118$ ($a = 199$, $b = -118$), where H is in meters (m). For $H = 1.70$ m, the forecast by the function is $W = 109 \times 1.7 - 118 = 67.3$ kg.

Now let us consider a more complex example.

Analysis of COVID-19 pandemic data

In 2020-2021, COVID-19 pandemic raged throughout the world. Let us take the pandemic in India as the sample data. In India, in the first 120 days, the total number of infections, denoted by $I(t)$, reached around 600,000. Here t is time in days from the beginning of the epidemic.

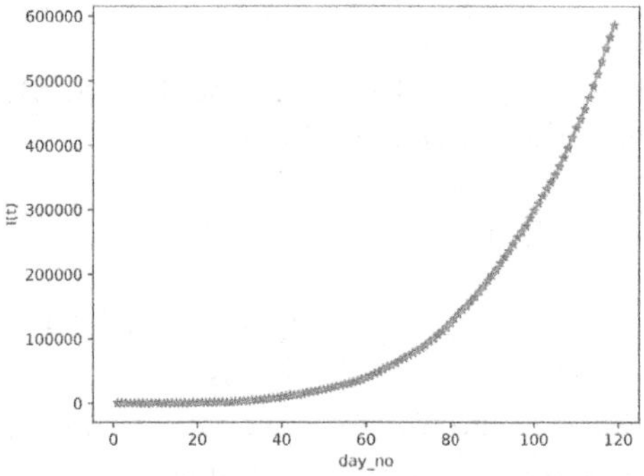

Figure 50: Plot of the total number of infections $I(t)$ vs. t (day_no) for COVID-19 epidemic in India

Hospitals and government agencies have recorded $I(t)$, which is available in various websites including https://www.worldometers.info/coronavirus/. We put this data in a file *'all.txt'* in two columns: the first column is t in days, and the second column is $I(t)$. Using the following Python script, we read the data, and then make a plot and print it in a pdf file *'india_all.pdf'*. See Section 11.2 for more details on the plot functions. The resulting plot is shown in Figure 50.

```
In [18]: all_data = loadtxt('all.txt')
```

```
In [23]: plot(all_data[:,0], all_data[:,1])
Out[23]: [<matplotlib.lines.Line2D at 0x7fcb0c32dcd0>]

In [24]: xlabel('day_no'); ylabel('I(t)')
Out[24]: Text(12.097222222222216, 0.5, 'I(t)'.

In [27]: savefig('india_all.pdf')
```

Clearly, $I(t)$ is not a simple function of t. A careful analysis shows that the $I(t)$ curve is a combination of an exponential function (from day 4 to day 27) and a polynomial (from day 63 to day 105). The region from day 28 to day 62 is the transition zone from the exponential function to the polynomial. In the following discussion we illustrate how to analyse these regions using Python. We remark that the above function has been arrived at by trial and error.

First we focus on the exponential regime of the plot where

$$I(t) = Ae^{at}.$$

A question, however, is how to determine the constants A and a. Taking a logarithm of the above equation yields

$$y = log(I(t)) = a\,t + \log(A) = a\,t + b. \quad \ldots(1)$$

The constants a and b can be easily determined by function *polyfit()*, which is part of the *Numpy* module. In particular, we employ *polyfit(t, y,1)*. The last argument of the function indicates that we are looking for a fit with first-order polynomial, $at + b$. That is,

```
p = polyfit(t,y,1)
```

The function returns an array p = array([0.16077067, 2.85035717]) with $a = p[0] = 0.16077067$ and $b = p[1] = 2.85035717$. Hence, the fit function is

$$y \approx log(I(t)) \approx 0.16\,t + 2.8. \quad \ldots(2)$$

In the above expression, we express the numbers up to two *significant digits*. Note that in a real number, the number of nonzero digits and zeros between the extreme non-zero digits is called *significant digits*. For example, the real numbers 10.3, 10.300, 010.30 have three significant digits. The zeros of the integer part prior to the first nonzero digit is ignored. In addition, we also ignore the zeros in the fraction beyond the last nonzero digit.

In Figure 51 we plot the linear fit of Eq. (2) along with the data. Note that many data points (shown as dots) are either above or below the best-fit curve (solid curve); these deviations are the error in the fit. Since we have only 24 data points in Figure 51, there are significant errors in a and b. However, in this book, we do not describe how to determine errors in a and b.

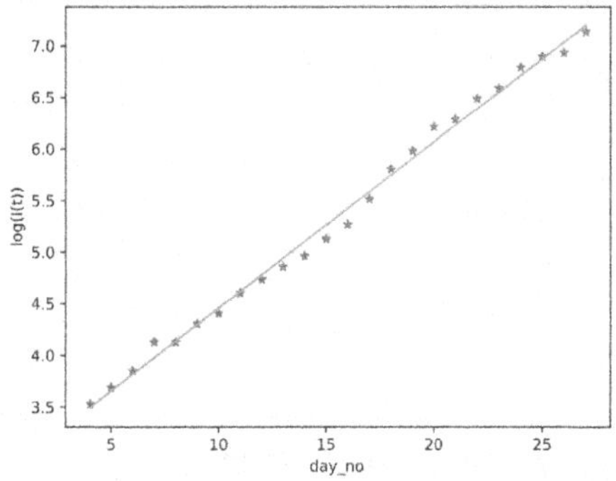

Figure 51: Plot of $log(I(t))$ vs. t for the exponential regime of the epidemic curve for which $a\ t + b$ (the straight line) is a good fit to the data (dots).

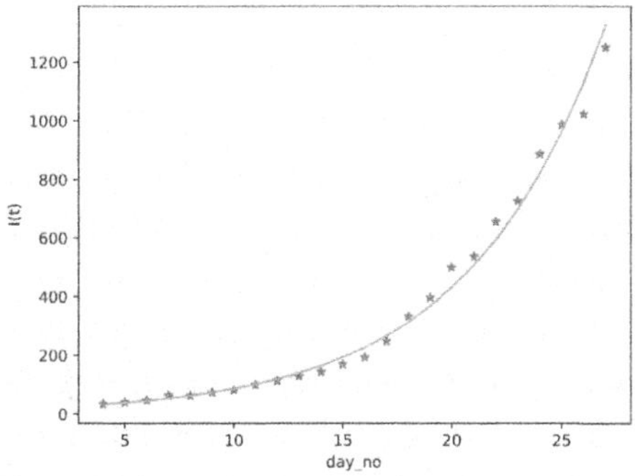

Figure 52: Plot of $I(t)$ vs. t for the exponential regime of the epidemic curve indicating that $I(t) = A\ e^{at}$ (the solid curve).

Using Eq. (2) we can derive that

$$I(t) \approx e^b\ e^{at} \approx 17\ e^{0.16t}.$$

In Figure 52 we plot *I*(*t*) vs. *t* that exhibits the exponential variation of *I*(*t*). The Python code used for the plotting and fitting the data is given below:

```
from numpy import *
from matplotlib.pyplot import *

# For the data that exhibits exponetial growth

figure()
exp_data = loadtxt('exp.txt')

t = exp_data[:,0]
y = log(exp_data[:,1])
p=polyfit(t,y,1)
y_fit = p[0]*t + p[1]

#  p = array([0.16077067, 2.85035717])

plot(t, y, '*')
plot(t, y_fit)
xlabel('day_no'); ylabel('log(I(t))')
savefig('india_exp_in_logy.pdf')

figure()
plot(t, exp_data[:,1], '*')
plot(t, exp(y_fit))
xlabel('day_no'); ylabel('I(t)')
savefig('india_exp.pdf')
```

Next, we consider the higher order polynomial of the epidemic curve; this regime is from day 63 to day 105. For this segment of data, we fit a second-order polynomial using the function *polyfit*(*t*, *z*, 2), where *t* and *z* are the arrays containing day and *I*(*t*) respectively. Note that *polyfit*() provides polynomials that are more general than linear function, hence it is a very useful function for modelling complex systems. A code segment for the polynomial fit is given below.

```
t = quad_data[:,0]
z = quad_data[:,1]
p = polyfit(t,z,2)
z_fit = p[0]*t**2 + p[1]*t + p[2]
```

The above code yields

p = array([1.18114516e+02, −1.25940874e+04, 3.76049563e+05]).

From the above function we deduce that

$$I(t) = 1.18114516e{+}02\ t^2 - 1.25940874e{+}04\ t + 3.76049563e{+}05.$$

However, we express the constants using three significant digits that yields

$$I(t) \approx 118\ t^2 - 12600\ t + 376000,$$

which is a quadratic function. This function, plotted in Figure 53, shows that the best-fit curve models the data (shown as dots) quite well.

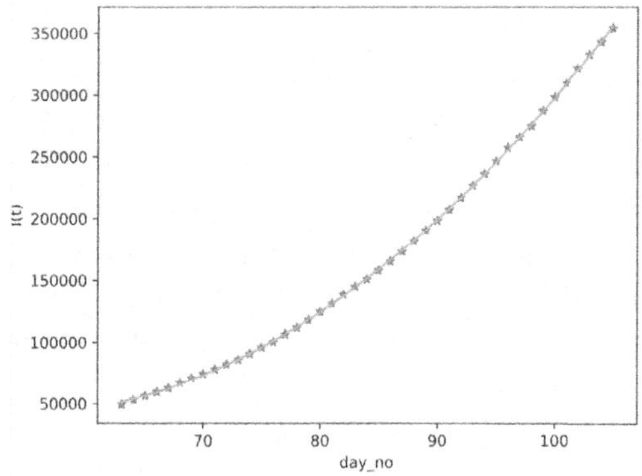

Figure 53: Plot of $I(t)$ vs. t for the polynomial regime of the epidemic curve. The best fit curve is $I(t) = 118\ t^2 - 12600t + 376000$.

To carry out our analysis further, in Figure 54, we plot $I(t)$ vs. t in *loglog* scale in which the best-fit curve is a straight line with slope of 3.9. That is, $\log(I(t)) \approx 3.9 \log(t) + B$. Therefore, $I(t) \approx 0.0047\ t^{3.9}$. A Python code for the analysis of the above power-law regime is given below.

```
loglog(t, z, '*')
loglog(t, z_fit)
z_fit2 = z[0]*(t/t[0])**3.9
loglog(t, z_fit2)
xlabel('day_no'); ylabel('I(t)')
savefig('india_quad_in_loglog.pdf')
```

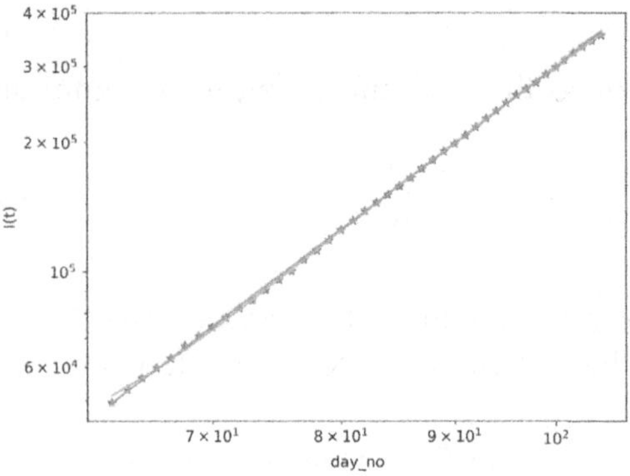

Figure 54: Plot of $I(t)$ vs. t for the polynomial regime in *loglog* scale shows that $I(t) \approx 0.0047\, t^{3.9}$.

With this, we end our preliminary discussion on the analysis of COVID-19 epidemic data.

In this section we discussed linear regression, as well as polyfit function of Python, that helps us determine linear and nonlinear functions that fit with the data. This technique is very useful for modelling complex systems, for example, COVID-19 epidemic, stock market, population growth, etc.

****

Exercises

1. You can download the COVID-19 infection data for the most-affected countries (e.g., USA, India, Brazil, UK, Italy) from *https://www.worldometers.info/coronavirus*. Following the procedure given in this section, work out the best-fit curves to

the epidemic curves for these countries.

2. Download the population data for India from *https://www.worldometers.info/world-population/india-population*. Plot the yearly data and derive the best-fit curves. Do the same analysis for the world data.

13.2 Artificial Intelligence and Machine Learning

Artificial intelligence (*AI*) and *machine learning* (*ML*) are being heavily applied to many areas of science and engineering. Unfortunately, AI and ML cannot be discussed in this introductory book. In the following discussion, we illustrate applications of AI using several examples.

Some AI programs help computers recognise characters. Such applications are used in the postal department for reading hand-written addresses, and in the income tax department for reading the income-tax return forms.

Let us explore how a character-recognition program works. First, a computer learns the characters using sample data. For example, we supply the computers with many hand-written characters with their identification. Such samples, called *training cases*, could be in thousands. Computer learns better with more and varied training cases. After training, the computer is ready for testing. We provide test cases to the computer, and test if the computer recognises the characters accurately. If yes, the program is ready for deployment. After such training, it is expected that the computer would do a good job in real-life situations.

Figure 55: Sample of numeral characters (0-9) that could be used for training a computer for character recognition. From MNIST database of wikipedia. Source wikipedia.org.

Figure 55 illustrates a sample of numeral characters that could be used for training and testing computers for character recognition. The present table contains 160 characters (note that we need much more data to train the machine).

Another example is how to contrast apple and oranges using computers. We train the computer using a large number of of apple and oranges. It has been observed that such programs accurately identify the fruits. This scheme works for real fruits, as well as for their images.

There are many more AI applications. Some of them are

- Speech to text conversion. *Youtube* often generates subtitles in movies using such applications.
- Language translations, e.g., English $\longleftrightarrow$ French
- Self-driving cars
- In piloting of aeroplanes
- E-marketing, as in amazon
- Weather forecasting

With these introductory remarks we close our discussion on machine learning and artificial intelligence.

Summary

Now, we are at the end of this book, which may possibly be your first programming book. This book provides a brief introduction to the following topics:

1. What is a computer?
2. Number system with an emphasis on binary system
3. How to install Python on your computer?
4. Introduction to Python programming
5. Using Python to solve computational problems
6. School mathematics (analysis, geometry) using Python
7. Introduction to data analysis and machine learning

Most of the above topics are vast with volumes written on them. This book is a first stepping stone to these topics, written with an aim to enthuse you to learn programming and advanced topics of science.

Programming is great fun! It is like creating music, poetry, or painting. We write a code to solve a problem, as well as for creative satisfaction. In some sense, we compose a program just like music. For all such activities we need to think clearly before we set out to create them. In programming, first, we solve the problem; second, we write the steps (called algorithm); and, finally, we write the code. After that, the code must be tested using a wide range of test cases. The program is ready only after these operations. We do hope that you experience the joy of programming after finishing this book.

Also, programming is like swimming or cycling. One cannot theorise such activities. You learn these skills by practice. Hence, we strongly recommend that you program! Don't just read a programming book! For Python programming, you could use your own computer, or use internet platforms such as Python Notebooks, Prutor, etc. We plan to offer a Python course for school students on Prutor (https://prutor.ai/mkvatiitkanpur/#)

In addition, explore materials on the internet. We provide some references at the end of this book, but internet has much more. You will get tons of material just by googling prime number, machine learning, linear regression, searching algorithms.

Needless to say that computer programming is one of the most important activities at present times. In addition to creative satisfaction, programming skills also offers you economic opportunities in terms of jobs. We wish you luck for becoming an excellent programmer.

Difficult Exercises

The following exercises are more difficult than the exercises given at the end of each section. Spend sometime thinking about these problems and and then solve them on computers using Python.

1. Write a computer program to discover positions of 4 queens on a 4x4 chess board so that the queens do not kill each other. List all the possible solutions.
2. Solve problem 1 for 8 queens on a 8x8 chess board.
3. *Knight's tour*: Consider a 4x4 chess board. Write a computer program to construct knight tour such that the knight visits every square of the board exactly once. List all possible solutions.
4. Solve problem 3 for the knight on 8x8 chess board.
5. We have 4 coins with one among them being heavier than the rest. Write a computer program to identify the defective coin using the least number of weighings. Make a tree diagram for the solution. **Hint:** For 4 coins, weigh coins 1 and 2 on one side, and coins 2 and 3 on the other side.
6. Generalize Exercise 5 for 8 coins.
7. Generalize Exercise 5 for 12 coins.
8. We have 4 coins among which one of them is defective (could be lighter or heavier). How will you identify the defective coin?
9. Do Exercise 8 for 8 coins and 12 coins.
10. Find the first 10000 prime numbers from the internet (for example, http://mathforum.org/dr.math/faq/faq.prime.num.html). Let us label them as P_n. Plot P_n vs. n. Also plot $P_{n+1} - P_n$ vs. n. Fit the second plot with $log(n)$.

References

Books

1. J. Briggs, *Python for Kids*, No Starch Press (2013).
2. B. Payne, *Teach Your Kids to Code*, No Starch Press (2015).
3. B. Scott, *Python for Kids*, John Wiley & Sons (2015).

Internet resources

1. *Colab*: https://colab.research.google.com
2. *Jupyter*: https://jupyter.org
1. *Anaconda*: https://www.anaconda.com
2. *Matplotlib*: https://matplotlib.org
3. *Numpy*: https://numpy.org

Subject Index

Subject Index

Made in the USA
Monee, IL
04 November 2026

67377506R00115